Modeling Servant-Leaders for Africa

Zapf Chancery Tertiary Level Publications

A Guide to Academic Writing by C. B. Peter (1994)
Africa in the 21st Century by Eric M. Aseka (1996)
Women in Development by Egara Kabaji (1997)
Introducing Social Science: A Guidebook by J. H. van Doorne (2000)
Elementary Statistics by J. H. van Doorne (2001)
Iteso Survival Rites on the Birth of Twins by Festus B. Omusolo (2001)
The Church in the New Millennium: Three Studies in the Acts of the Apostles by John Stott (2002)
Introduction to Philosophy in an African Perspective by Cletus N. Chukwu (2002)
Participatory Monitoring and Evaluation by Francis W. Mulwa and Simon N. Nguluu (2003)
Applied Ethics and HIV/AIDS in Africa by Cletus N. Chukwu (2003)
For God and Humanity: 100 Years of St. Paul's United Theological College Edited by Emily Onyango (2003)
Establishing and Managing School Libraries and Resource Centres by Margaret Makenzi and Raymond Ongus (2003)
Introduction to the Study of Religion by Nehemiah Nyaundi (2003)
A Guest in God's World: Memories of Madagascar by Patricia McGregor (2004)
Introduction to Critical Thinking by J. Kahiga Kiruki (2004)
Theological Education in Contemporary Africa edited by GrantLeMarquand and Joseph D. Galgalo (2004)
Looking Religion in the Eye edited by Kennedy Onkware (2004)
Computer Programming: Theory and Practice by Gerald Injendi (2005)
Demystifying Participatory Development by Francis W. Mulwa (2005)
Music Education in Kenya: A Historical Perspective by Hellen A. Odwar (2005)
Into the Sunshine: Integrating HIV/AIDS into Ethics Curriculum Edited by Charles Klagba and C. B. Peter (2005)
Integrating HIV/AIDS into Ethics Curriculum: Suggested Modules Edited by Charles Klagba (2005)
Dying Voice (An Anthropological Novel) by Andrew K. Tanui (2006)
Participatory Learning and Action (PLA): A Guide to Best Practice by Enoch Harun Opuka (2006)
Science and Human Values: Essays in Science, Religion, and Modern Ethical Issues edited by Nehemiah Nyaundi and Kennedy Onkware (2006)
Understanding Adolescent Behaviour by Daniel Kasomo (2006)
Students' Handbook for Guidance and Counselling by Daniel Kasomo (2007)
BusinessOrganization and Management: Questions and Answers by Musa O. Nyakora (2007)

(Continued on page 200)

Modeling Servant-Leaders for Africa
LESSONS FROM ST. PAUL

Ven. Ndung'u John Brown Ikenye,
PhD, DMin
Senior Lecturer in Counseling Psychology and Practical Theology
St. Paul's University, Limuru, Kenya

Zapf Chancery
Eldoret, Kenya

First Published 2010
© Ndung'u John Brown Ikenye
All rights reserved.

Cover Concept and Design
C. B. Peter

Associate Designer and Typesetter
Nancy Njeri

Copyediting
Charles M. Ngugi, PhD
Joseph Galgalo, PhD

Editor and Publishing Consultant
C. B. Peter

Printed by
Kijabe Printing Press,
P. O. Box 40,
Kijabe.

Published by

Zapf Chancery Research Consultants and Publishers,
P. O. Box 4988,
Eldoret, Kenya.
Email: zapfchancerykenya@yahoo.co.uk
Mobile: 0721-222 311

ISBN 978-9966-7341-8-1

This book has been printed on fully recyclable, environment-friendly paper.

To The Rt. Rev. Dr. Gideon Githiga and fellow Clergy and Laity,
Called and Sent to the Ministry of Servant-Leadership in Kenya and the wider world

In Memory of
The Most Rev. Dr. Manasses Kuria, Bishop of Nakuru, and later served as Archbishop of Kenya and Bishop of Nairobi

Foreword

By The Rev. Canon Prof. Joseph D. Galgalo

Although there is a phenomenal growth in the churches in Kenya today, there is also a deep gulf between our confession of faith and practical commitment to what we profess. The numerical strength is by no means a reflection of quality church growth and neither is 'growth' always translated into any meaningful transformation of society. The gap 'servant leaders' necessary for a dynamic qualitative growth guided by clear vision, between faith and practice is attributable to a variety of factors but key among this is the aridity of purpose and sacrificial service. One consequence of this is that we are engulfed by myriad of challenges inimical to the very health of our Christianity.

Dr. Ikenye's book is timely and spot on in pointing out these varied challenges. The church is vibrant and alive and the strong presence of the church is worth celebrating. But the self-authenticating nominal Christianity, that has become a happy captive to an extremely materialistic-worldly culture, characterized by deplorable social inequalities, negative ethnicity and greed for power, among other setbacks, constitutes the proverbial fly in the ointment. No one expects the church to attain absolute perfection, at least not in any complete sense before the final consummation. What is contended with is a Christianity that has comfortably become at home in this world and by its worldly character compromises the true mission of the church. Conformity is what is here seen as the malady. It is in this light that two helpful recommendations are offered: redefining mission as the all embracing activity of God, to be understood and applied in its holistic, transformative and inclusive sense, as well as adopting a leadership whose character and ethos are modeled on biblical principles.

In addressing these issues, this book offers a thorough exploration of biblical and theological foundations of church growth. Leadership models of Jesus and that of Paul are ably expounded and presented as the basis for the argument that: effective, sustainable and quality church growth can be realized if the church today is led by servant leaders who are well grounded in the principles afforded by these models. Integrity, commitment and selfless service are particularly emphasized as the hallmark of godly, successful leaders who by their life and ministry can bring about transformation and the extension of the Kingdom of God. The outward, visible expression of such success is the 'quality' of church growth measured against the church's life-changing, transformative engagements. While qualities and values of servant leadership can be caught and nurtured, it is here also argued that adequate and relevant training to equip godly servant-leaders is absolutely necessary. Accordingly, each chapter, one after the other, is replete with examples and practical tips of how meaningful success may be achieved in church growth. In my view, it is with regard to this last point that the particular strength and value of this study lies.

Prof. Joseph D. Galgalo
Vice Chancellor
St. Paul's University, Limuru

Foreword

By Bishop Gideon Githiga, PhD

I am privileged to have been requested by the Ven. Dr. John Ikenye to write a forward of his invaluable book on "Church Growth and Servant Leadership." Dr. Ikenye is both a senior lecturer at St Paul's University, Limuru and the Archdeacon in charge of Human Development in the Diocese of Thika. I have severally listened to his lectures to both the clergy and the laity of my Diocese. The book is a fulfillment of the desire of his audience to have something they can refer to after his talks.

The author attempts to bring together theory and practice in the two institutions as he teaches and interacts intensively with all levels of Christians, from the university to the local church. The write demonstrates that church growth and leadership go hand in hand. Poor leadership slows growth and sometimes leads to division and hence the mushrooming of too many denominations in Kenya.

Dr. Ikenye traces the growth of the Kenyan church from the missionary/colonial era, through Independence to the present time. He argues that leadership was transferred from the missionary to African leadership in hasty manner. This led to some challenges like finances, lack of adequate theological training and constant divisions due to poor leadership. The research however appreciates that notwithstanding these challenges, the young church started moving toward self-ruling, self-supporting and self-propagation.

He attributes the growth of the Kenyan church to political stability, co-operation among denominations, enhanced theological training, empowered youth ministry, rising level of literacy and encouragement of priesthood of all believers. But there are visible challenges that go with a growing church. Leadership for example takes different directions as it manifests itself in a pluralistic society. In some communities, the church leader takes the stance of a tribal chief or king where he is treated with immense respect. If unchecked, this type of leadership may lead to abuse of office including financial mismanagement and oppression of the clergy and the laity by the person at the top. He argues that church leadership can only overcome the challenge by getting rid of ethnocentrism.

Other challenges include lack of enough qualified clergy to cope with the rate of growth of the congregations. Where a priest looks after up to ten congregations, he exercises too much delegation to untrained lay leaders. This type of leadership may make the priest to exercise excess authority or in retrospect make the laity gang against his leadership. This usually brings about conflicts and misunderstanding that hinder church growth.

Dr Ikenye appreciates lay leadership, but also emphasizes the need to have the leaders trained. He notes that high rate of denominational split is as a result of inadequate training of leaders or lack of it. This sometimes leads to conflict, hatred, mistrust and financial struggle.

In his book the author encourages his readers to adopt the New Testament model of leadership. In the gospels, Jesus demonstrated leadership by the washing of his disciples' feet, a sign of humility. This is where the author is getting the sub-title of his book, "Servant Leadership." Then "Church Growth" starts at the Great Commission. In the Pauline epistles, Paul argues that "Church Growth" and ideal leadership starts at personal encounter with Christ. One cannot exercise leadership in the church if he does not have self encounter with Christ and is clothed with his humility. This type of leadership is then guided by the Holy Spirit and is devoid of self-edification and enhances church growth.

Dr. Ikenye finally emphasizes on the need of improved training at all levels. He advises church leaders to create mechanisms of careful scrutiny on candidates applying for theological training and before the same are qualified for ordination. He argues that leaders should be beyond reproach for effective church leadership and growth.

There could be nothing more original and pragmatic on practical ministry than this research by the Ven. Dr. John Ikenye. I recommend all church leaders and those aspiring to be leaders to read it.

Rt. Rev. Dr. Gideon Githiga
Bishop
Diocese of Thika
Anglican Church of Kenya

Foreword

By Mark R. Ramseth

Modeling Servant-Leaders for Africa: Lessons from St. Paul expands the vision of the evangelical outreach in churches and congregations. What catches my attention is the potential this book offers for bridging continents in a common voice of mission outreach. Dr. Ikenye's book intimately links me, the reader, with the Church in Africa in evangelical witness. On a recent trip to St. Paul's University, Limuru, Kenya, I visited Dr. Ikenye and found an immediate bond of commonality on mission, and a common acknowledgement in the call of African churches to reach out with a new witness of vitality and sprit to brothers and sisters of the Gospel around the Globe.

In his Modeling *Servant-Leaders for Africa: Lessons from St. Paul,* Dr. Ikenye breaks paradigms of the first generation (the "missionary church-growth centered leadership"—a Western paradigm) and invites an encounter into new and hopeful ways for bringing Pauline modes of servant-leadership into the witness of the congregation. This book offers encouragement to the larger church in a changing world for bringing the Word of Christ anew.

As an American Christian invested in the ministry of the Gospel and theological education, and with a long vocation history of mission development in the United States, might I offer the prospect that

Jesus who was faithfully brought to one continent in another century, can now be "returned" in new vital ways to those who originally brought him.

Read this book!

Mark R. Ramseth
President
Trinity Lutheran Seminary
Columbus, Ohio, USA

Preface

The tremendous church growth witnessed in Kenya can be attributed to the wise leadership of the Kenyans who took over leadership roles from the missionaries. Their success shows commitment to mission and hard work in growing an African Christian church. The growth shows empowerment by the Holy Spirit as the motivating force. Unfortunately, Africans who are interdependent by nature, also inherited the Western systems of thinking, behaving, relating and the core values of independence and self-reliance. African Christian leadership has shown, not only length without depth, but also a leadership without much accountability to those led. As the church leaders face the hindrances of church growth, they are challenged in this book to engage in what I describe as the third revolution.

The first revolution was that of taking the church from the missionaries. This system of indigenization and Africanization brought blessings and challenges to church growth. The blessing was reflected in increased membership through evangelism. The challenge has been that of raising servant leaders. This book contains an extensive study on the subject of servant leadership in the New Testament.

The hindrances of church growth in Africa are expressed in the following two proverbs of Agikuyu and Waswahili of Kenya. The Agikuyu proverb states: *"Iri guthua ndongoria itikinyagira nyeki."* Translated, it means that "once the leader weakens, low morale follows," or "when the leader fails, all those who follow him or her are also doomed to fail."

The Waswahili have a similar proverb, "*mgema akisifiwa pombe hulitia maji*" translated it means," when you praise a brewer, he/she adds water to the brew," meaning, "too much praise can ruin effective leadership".

The common sentiment among theological students interviewed during this research was that, the higher you go into church leadership positions, the colder you become toward clergy and laity.

These two proverbs and student sentiment seem to describe a real situation as far as some of the church leaders in Kenya are concerned. These proverbs also serve as explicit warnings to church leaders to be careful in their leadership styles, lest they fail those that they lead. Such failure becomes a hindrance of church growth.

Worldliness has entered the church. We see headlines in newspapers of quarrels and misunderstanding between church leaders. There are church councils and individual church leaders who have leadership problems. The media has been used as the medium of squaring the scores. Quarrels and misunderstanding between bishops, moderators, clergy and laity are in the public domain. There is a leadership crisis, especially when church leaders become tribal chiefs. This book analyses and discusses in detail the manifest and latent meaning of leadership problems as hindrances to church growth.

In recent times, church leaders as servants of God and the people have used confrontation instead of dialogue to resolve disputes within the church. This book discusses systems of conflict transformation for the purposes of church growth.

To reverse the foregoing trends, this book seeks to help the African Christian leaders to follow the notions of biblical leadership as servanthood. What I understand as the challenge of the churches in Kenya and Africa is to train men and women with biblical and academic knowledge, which will be critical, practical, pastoral and applicable in the Kenyan context. It is also necessary to train men and women to participate in the discovery, transmission and preservation of knowledge and stimulate the intellectual life and cultural development of Kenya.

The Bible gives us the model of church leadership; hence, this book dwells on biblical principles of leadership. The book also utilizes non-biblical principles of leadership in the discussion and discovery, so long as such texts do not contradict biblical principles.

Finally, the book explores the dynamics of balanced church growth as the church moves into the third revolution of church growth. The church grows in the world and in community. We cannot speak about church growth in Kenya without speaking about the political systems that affect church, in hindering or fostering the contexts for growth in the nation. Servant leadership as addressed in this book most also speak to political readers. I commend this book to church and political leaders, all given servanthood as a call to serve the people of God.

Acknowledgements

The congregations that I have served in various capacities over the past 30 years have given me the basic challenges that resulted into writing the present book. The Anglican Church of Kenya (ACK) Diocese of Thika, where I presently serve, has 158 parishes. Their ministries under the leadership of The Rt. Rev. Dr. Gideon Githiga have also given me an opportunity to teach some of the materials presented in this book. To all clergy and laity who have contributed to the learning the dynamics of church growth, I owe you with gratitude.

The materials in the second section of this book were first researched while I was at Nairobi International School of Theology. I owe with gratitude, the faculty and staff, especially Dr. A. Scott Moreau, Rev. Gary A. Fredrick, Clarence Ben Sorrels and Dr. Lazarus Seruyange. I also thank the staff and faculty of Pan Africa Christian College (now Pan African Christian University) where I had my first courses in Evangelism and Church Growth. They planted a seed that has continued to grow over the years.

I have dedicated this book to The Most Rev. Dr. Manasses Kuria, my first mentor and bishop, whom I loved and saw as a role model. The late Manasses remained faithful and passionate to the Gospel, and saw its power to change lives. His commitment to planting and growing churches, in the dioceses of Nakuru and Nairobi will be remembered for generations. He was the founder of Diocesan Missionary Associations, in the Province and a leader of distinction who grew the Church in his exemplary life and practice of ministry.

Last but not least, these materials are a revision of my lecture-notes originally presented to students of "Church growth" at Garrett-Evangelical Theological Seminary, Seabury-Western Theological Seminary and St. Paul's University. I thank them for their contributions and critique of the materials presented in this book. They provided a context for formation and learning together.

When writing this book, I spent more time alone in my house office and the one at St. Paul's University. At home this meant less time with Rose Njeri Ndung'u, my wife. I thank her for understanding, love and patience, faithfully endured. For the faculty, it meant less time around the hallways and at the staff lounge. I thank them for their understanding, gracious support, and encouraging words.

I am deeply grateful to my senior colleague the Rev. Canon Prof Joseph Galgalo, Vice Chancellor, St. Paul's University, for his ardent work in copyediting and also providing valuable peer-review and critique to help me improve the present book.

Finally, to my editor, the Rev. Christopher Peter, I say *thank you* for his relentless encouragement and editorial consultancy to the entire project and keeping me focused. He has published this book as a gift to myself and the readers.

Introduction

The task of learning the theory and practice of church growth as presented in this book began with my conversion to Christianity from African Traditional Religion of the Agikuyu on 14 April 1974. The joy and excitement of knowing Christ and joining the Christian community at St. Christopher's, Nakuru brought a passion for the Church. I saw and experienced the local church as the ideal community of love. From this experience I was involved in planting and growing the church at Nakuru Blankets Factory and Kabatini as out stations of Menengai Parish. This parish covered Njoro and Northern parts of Nakuru. After my ordination as a priest on 23 December 1979, I was posted to Nyandarua Parish, and stationed at Wanjohi Town Center, and as a curate to Venerable Ladan Kamau, who later became bishop of the diocese of Nakuru. The parish covered Dondori area, Ol'Kalau and Kipipiri areas, with 21 congregations. The experiences of growing church with vast areas required the clergy to work closely with laity. On 1st January 1980, I became a curate at St. Stephen's Church, Jogoo Road. The metropolitan parish had a membership of 4,500. With congregations meeting at 7.30am, 9.30am, 10.30am and 6.30pm, the growth of the church depended on us three clergy and a vast number of laity. The parish council members were evangelists in their own right. It was during this year that I was also involved in planting church at Embakasi and Soweto Village and Nairobi South C.

In 1982, these two areas became parishes, leaving St. Stephen's standing on its own. While Rev. Moses Ndung'u went to Embakasi and Soweto, I remained at St. Paul's Nairobi South as its first Vicar.

Rose Njeri Ndung'u, my wife and served this parish until August 1988, when I left for Evanston, USA, for further studies. Upon my departure, due to the numerical growth of the parish,
St. Paul's was divided into two parishes, giving birth to St. Monica's Parish, South B.

In August 1988, I joined St. Mark's Parish, Evanston, Illinois, USA as an Assisting Priest. While I attended Garrett-Evangelical Theological Seminary, I was not only involved with St. Mark's, I visited Methodist, Lutheran and Presbyterian Churches as way of learning and serving the church.

In October of 1990, I became Associate Vicar at The Church of the Epiphany, Chicago. This small congregation, with a school for boys gave me an opportunity to do evangelism among the African Americans living in "Housing Projects". This "Inner City" experience added to the methods of growing church beyond boundaries of age, race, gender and culture. The growth of this parish opened an opportunity to serve the church at St. Andrew's, Evanston from 16 June 1993 to 4th June 2006. This international congregation with 15 nations represented in the membership opened my eyes to cross-cultural dynamics of church growth.

The postcolonial church growth in Kenya can be attributed to the wise leadership of Kenyans who took over leadership roles from the missionaries. Their success shows empowerment by the Holy Spirit. Brining people to Christ for redemption has been a commitment to both the missionaries and African Christian leaders. Their second commitment has been to helping Christians to grow in fellowship in a close walk with Christ and with one another. Their third commitment has been to developing Christians for responsible church membership and a holistic and wholistic membership of the Church. Unfortunately, the Christian leaders of the first generation also inherited the Western systems of thinking, behaving, relating and the core values of independence and self-reliance without accountability to those lead. The present book focuses on methods and principles of church growth. The book is a critique of the first Christian generation paradigm of church growth and its leadership, but also encourages and challenges church leaders to understand and face the hindrances of church growth without fear. Church growth as an intentional process requires putting together synergies under the leadership of the Holy Spirit. All church leaders are challenged in this book to engage in engaging the third revolution as they reflect on the strengths, passion and weaknesses of the first and second revolutions of church growth in Kenya. The baseline is that, missionaries who embarked on planting the church in Kenya, had the passion and commitment for the propagation of the Gospel. They used methods and principles of the missionary and biblical paradigms with their hearts in the forefront. The first section of this book focuses on methods and principles of church growth, know to have been used effectively in Kenya. This first section also seeks to understand church mission, and biblical-theological models of church growth.

Church growth in Kenya has also to be understood in terms of revolutions. The first revolution was that of taking the church from the missionaries. This system of indigenization and Africanization brought both blessings and challenges to church growth. The blessing was an increase in membership through evangelism. One to one methods of preaching, and crusades were used to attract members to the new "Christ Movement." The challenge has been that of raising servant leaders. The second part of this book has an extensive study on the subject of servant leadership in the New Testament. The idea of this second section is that the message and messenger go hand in hand, mainly as servant and as leader. Church growth is empowered by both sides of the coin, as used by the Holy Spirit.

The hindrances of church growth in Africa are expressed in the following two proverbs of Agikuyu and Waswahili of Kenya.

The Agikuyu have a proverb, *"Iri guthua ndungoria itikinyagira nyeki,"* ("Once the leader weakens, lost morale follows," or "when the leader fails, all those who follow him or her are also doomed to fail.")

The Waswahili have a similar proverb, *"ukimsifu mgema atia pombe maji,"* ("When you praise the brewer, he or she may spoil the brew by adding water to it," meaning that, too much praise can ruin effective leadership.)

The common sentiment among theological students interviewed at St. Paul's University, in the regular and parallel program, and a large cadre of Christians and leaders interviewed during this research was that the higher you go into church leadership positions, the colder you become toward clergy and laity, except only to the rich and your protectors and king-makers.

The two proverbs I mentioned above seem to apply to many of the church leaders in Kenya. These two proverbs also serve as explicit warnings to church leaders, to be careful in their leadership styles, lest they fail those that they lead. Such failure becomes a hindrance to church growth. Jamlick Muchangi Miano, a student at the Bachelor of Divinity in 1980, St. Paul's United Theological College and now a Minister in the Presbyterian Church of East Africa wrote a book entitled, *Hyenas in the Church*, calling on church leaders to reform leadership styles and leadership in the church as a whole.[1] Bishop Gideon Githiga, of the Anglican Diocese of Thika, in *Effective Church Leadership*, calls for professional pastoral church leadership from the underground, for both laity and clergy.[2] Church growth cannot be separated from servant leadership because it is based on the biblical premise that the message and the messenger are inseparable.

It would hardly require any formal documentation to prove that today worldliness has entered into the church. We see frequent headlines in newspapers of quarrels and misunderstanding between church leaders. Various church councils and individual church leaders have leadership problems, often traceable to personality-battles or tribal politicking. But conceited leaders opt for settling their personal scores through media-wars. Quarrels and misunderstanding between bishops, moderators, clergy often spill out into the public domain.

---

[1] Jamlick Muchangi Miano, *Hyenas in The Church*, Nairobi: Uzima Press, 1981.

[2] Gideon G. Githiga, *Effective Church Leadership*, Nairobi: Uzima Press, 2009.

There is a leadership crisis, especially when church leaders start behaving like tribal chiefs. This book takes a serious step of analyzing and discussing in detail the manifest and latent meaning of leadership problems as hindrances to church growth. Church leaders as servants of God and the people in recent times have used confrontation instead of dialogue to transform leadership problems of indiscipline. This book also discusses systems of conflict transformation for the purposes of church growth.

To change the trends above, this book seeks to help African Christian leaders to follow the notions of biblical leadership as servanthood. What I understand as the challenge of the churches in Kenya and Africa is to train men and women with biblical and academic knowledge. Towards that end, this book will help the Christian leader to be more critical, practical and pastoral in the practice of leadership. This book will also encourage Christian leaders to do self- reflection and self-supervision with more applicable issues in their context. It is also necessary to train men and women to participate in the discovery, transmission and preservation of knowledge and stimulate the intellectual life and cultural development. This book will encourage the leader in the journey of discovery, preservation, and development of new ways to understand and practice leadership.

The Bible gives us the model of church leadership; hence, this book dwells on biblical principles of leadership. The book also utilizes non-biblical principles of leadership in the discussion and discovery, as long as such texts do not contradict the biblical principles. The innovations and liberal thoughts of our times are bringing the sin of addition, subtraction, multiplication and complication while dealing with biblical texts. This book does biblical exegesis (study of Greek Texts and word usage) to avoid aisiogesis (putting or forcing meaning into words).

The book explores the dynamics of balanced church growth, to demonstrate the necessity of the church growth movement into the third revolution of church growth in the African context.

Contents

Foreword by Prof. Joseph Galgalo......................................*vii*
Foreword by Bishop Gideon Githiga, PhD..........................*ix*
Foreword by President Ramseth..*xiii*
Preface..*xv*
Acknowledgements..*xviii*
Introduction...*xx*

Part One: Leadership and Church Growth
Chapter One: Prophetic Leadership for
    Church Growth...3
Chapter Two: Defining Church Growth in the
    Context of Mission...9
Chapter Three: Basic Assumptions of
    Church Growth...21
Chapter Four: Biblical and Theological Foundations
    of Church Growth..27
Chapter Five: The Church as a System and
    Its Models...37
Chapter Six: Models of Church Growth: Jesus
    and Paul..47
Chapter Seven: Leadership Positions and Mission
    for Growth..55

Part Two: The New Testament Understanding of Leadership

Chapter Eight: Survey of the New Testament
Concept of Leadership..65

Chapter Nine: The New Testament Vocabulary
for Servant-Leadership..77

Chapter Ten: An Exegetical Examination
of Ephesians 4:1-6..95

Chapter Eleven: An Exegetical Examination
of I Timothy 3:1-16..115

Chapter Twelve: An Exegetical Examination
of Titus 1:1-16..133

Chapter Thirteen: Summary of the Pauline
Concept of Leadership...145

Part Three: Church Leadership: The Kenyan Experience

Chapter Fourteen: Church Leadership in Kenya:
An Overview...153

Chapter Fifteen: Church Leadership in Kenya in
Light of Biblical Principles...................................175

Part Four: Epilogue

Chapter Sixteen: Summary and Conclusion...................185

Recommended Bibliography......................................187

Part One: Leadership and Church Growth

CHAPTER ONE

Prophetic Leadership for Church Growth

Introduction

The church of our times needs servants and leaders who are prophets and prophetesses, who will proclaim openly and publicly the will of God for the church. The times are now, to develop a new crop of servant oriented leadership which will focus their hearts and mind on this unique moment in the history of the church. The present situation in the affairs of the world is a ripe time and opportunity for growing the church. This book is a prophetic book for church growth, in that, it seeks to proclaim and expound the theory and method of church growth, and God's intentions for leaders to be servants.

Prophetic leadership is not about prediction about the future of church, its leadership or its membership, rather it is telling and living the truth as revealed by the Word of God in Scripture. Prophesy also means preaching and teaching the Word of God with power, with the goal of telling the truth that sets people free, and equipping them for the works of service. Prophesy also involves discerning and distinguishing the spirits and voices, idols and demonic powers which make claims in the lives of the people of God. There are so many people today who claim to speak for God, but are speaking in the name of ego-centrism (as they personally see things) and ethno-centrism (as things are dictated by culture and ethnic communities). These two idols, of personal and cultural-ethnic idealization, must be encountered by prophetic church leadership. The encounter and empowerment of church leaders and ordinary Christians who are called to a priesthood of all believers is necessary for our times. These encounters have led and will lead to church growth. But church growth must also be done in strategic ways, using methods and strategies that will result in growth. All Christians must be involved in church planting, which I suggest must be done intentionally, strategically, empirically and methodically.

The African church has grown from the missionary era and ethos of reception and imposition. That sense of colonial Christianity and colonial church has been replaced by an Africanized and indigenized church leadership. This church growth has had male-dominated models of leadership, yet women are the majority members. What we see in our times is an African church which grows due to the inclusion of women in all cadres of servant leadership. The African church has grown from a monolithic church leadership that used to perform liturgy in Latin and English to an Africanized and multi-lingual church. This empowered church has grown and reached many in their ethnic communities. Ethnocentrism has plagued the church in many ways, with church leaders assuming the mantle of tribal chiefs. But, on the other hand, ethnocentric aspects such as language and music have made Christianity understandable, while at the same time exposing a nasty flipside. Demonization of ethnicity and culture in the missionary era led to division, fighting and a negative self-image. The struggles of this third revolution are to develop leaders who are bi-cultural, acculturated and inculturated. Some of the church leaders have been and continue to be egocentric, ethnocentric, and monocultural and jacks of all trade and masters of none. Quarrels, misunderstanding, locking of heads, corruption, financial scandals, immorality, tribalism, sectionalism, and nepotism are hindrances to church growth.

Democratization and politicization of the church is also a hindrance to church growth as the minority communities are excluded in church leadership and decision making. The new church growth by strategy requires that these minorities be seen as a mission field. In the name of " doing administration and being busy attitudes," some quarters of church leadership have developed a culture of mediocrity: do as I say and not as I do; fighting for higher offices in the church; playing of political games; reactionism and last minute actions, arrogance and self-righteousness, selfishness, and cramming for power, pride, prestige, and possessions, and prejudice. All these are hindrances to church growth. The problems of abuse and misuse of power are common hindrances of church growth. Misuse and misappropriation money and sexual immorality, just like olve money are known to be "clergy and laity killers" and to be detractors of church growth. Righteousness and holiness in life are necessities for church growth.

The new church growth strategy will be shown in this book to include both personality skills and character of living.[1] Emphasis of personality will include administrative skills, public image, attitudes and behaviors as part of what a leader brings into the ministry, as a gift for church growth. The productive ability and skills will contribute to the growth of the church. Character is also shown in the research of this book as integral to church growth. The servant and leader will need to be ethical. Ethical character is shown by integrity, humility, fidelity, temperance, courage, doing justice, simplicity, modesty and industry.

The African church emphasized knowing Christ in the first revolution. In the second revolution, the church formed a community of saints for the works of service and Africanized its leadership. This third revolution must grow a church of passionate and compassionate servant-leaders who will be responsible, service-driven, creative and loving, self-reliant and yet interdependent, and responsible and accountable to the community of saints. David Switzer suggests that, servant-leaders must: know and be aware of oneself (present to oneself); know Christ (a person of deep faith); a person of charisma (a humanizer, facilitator, professional, and expert-amateur) and a

---

[1] Stephen R. Covey, *The Seven Habits of the Highly Effective People*, New York: Simon & Schuster, 1989, 18-23. He focuses on restoring of character as an impetus for effective leadership.

person of mature emotional condition and attitude (accurate in empathy, interpathy, respect, and genuineness).[2] The fact that message and messenger go hand in hand, in church growth means that, personal, biblical, communal and professional qualifications must be emphasized in church growth methods. Kenyan churches are requiring of their leaders to be highly trained. Likewise, on-going nurturing of leaders is a new reality. The Anglican Church of Kenya, Diocese of Thika has a full-fledged department of human resources development, for lay and clergy training and leadership development. This department's core value is aligning of church leaders and ministries for personal and communal growth. For a period of three years, empowerment training programs for church leaders have proved to increase membership, financial support for ministry, satisfaction among members, and a sense of direction and purpose for parishes and diocese.

The African church of the third revolution which intends to grow in numbers and spiritual quality must focus on the five mission purposes[3] : worship (music and preaching which Afro-centric); pastoral ministerial functions for the African context; evangelism within and beyond its membership (going, baptizing and discipleship for maturing the saints for the works of service; build fellowship to enhance mid-week church and grow a sense of ownership and belonging; and discipleship that teaches spiritual depth, discernment and discipline.

The struggles of the third revolution must include developing bi-cultural, acculturated and enculturated servant-leaders. As bi-cultural persons, pastors and lay-leadership must be able to function

---

[2] David Switzer, *Pastor, Preacher and Person*, Nashville: Abingdon Press, 1979, 13-19.

[3] Rick Warren, *The Purpose Driven Church: Growth Without Compromising Your Message and Mission*, Grand Rapids, Michigan, 1995, 95-109, uses 1 Corinthians 1:10 to emphasize that a purpose driven church will grow by focusing on worship, ministry, evangelism, fellowship and discipleship.

within their ethnic and culture of origin but also be able to function within other ethnic and cultural boundaries. As acculturated servant-leaders, they must see the gifts of diversity in the church, rather than requiring uniformity. As enculturated servant-leaders, they must learn from other ethnic communities and cultures, for the purposes of growing an inclusive church.

Modeling for Servant Leadership

CHAPTER TWO

Defining Church Growth in the Context of Mission

Introduction

Church growth is defined with multiple dimensions due to the fact that there is not one thing that defines church growth. Church growth means different things as will be shown below, depending on the emphasis of the person defining and the dimensions of observation. For example, Warren, in his book, *The Purpose driven Church,1995* (p. 14), says several things about church growth: Only God makes the church to grow; only God can breathe new life into a valley of dry bones; only God can create waves - of revival, growth, and spiritual receptivity. This means that, the sovereignty of God is paramount to church growth. Our work in church growth is to recognize how God is working in the world and join Him in partnership. To grow the church, leaders have to recognize the waves, use the right resources that are God given and the right equipment in riding the God-given waves of growth, with a balance. This is what God was saying to the Corinthian church in 1Corinthians 3:16, that they are "God's temple," and are "indwelt" by the Holy Spirit. Warren's emphasis is God's activity in using servant-leaders for the growth of: warm fellowship; discipleship for depth; worship for strength; ministerial and pastoral functions for a broadened ministry; and growing a larger church in membership.

Jensen and Stevens, in their book, *Dynamics of Church Growth*, (1981) suggest that, church growth is balanced increase in quantity, quality, and organizational complexity of a local church.[1] It is growth by prayer, worship, purpose, analysis and diagnosis and prioritizing, planning and programming for evangelism, discipleship, fellowship among members, holistic and wholistic stewardship in a local congregation, diocese or presbytery. Growth of the church requires creating a climate for loving, serving, relating in mature ways, and development of leaders. Church growth is the experience of belonging, participating, loyalty and commitment.

Wagner in his book, *Your Church Can Grow,* (1976) defines church growth as all that which is involved in bringing men and women to a personal relationship with Jesus Christ, have fellowship with Him, and into responsible church membership.[2] Church growth is involving members in small groups (the church in the middle of the week) after training leaders for leading those groups, and equipping members for the works of service by building their knowledge, skills and character.

In defining church growth, we have to think of multiple aspects on the ministry and mission of the church. First, leaders are the point of focus. An Agikuyu proverb says: *iguthua ndungoria itingikinyira nyeki.* In every church, parish, diocese, or presbytery, there are servant-leaders who work together in realizing mission and ministry. Hence, in this book, I spend a considerable amount of space dealing with questions of leadership and servanthood as core aspects to church growth. Second, leaders work with God's grace and the empowerment of the Holy Spirit who has called then into the vineyard. Leaders and the church are signs of grace. Church growth has to do with realization of the church as a Sacrament. The

---

[1] Ron Jenson and Jim Stevens, *Dynamics of Church Growth*, Grand Rapids, Michigan: Baker Book House, 1981, 10.
[2] C. Peter Wagner, *Your Church Can Grow*, Glendale, California: Regal Books, 1976, 12.

church has to grow in showing the reality of God's grace and love shown in Christ. The church is the visible sign of the inner meaning of grace. This means that, servant-leaders must be models of the grace of God as shown in Christ.

Third, church growth involves discernment under the enlightenment of the Holy Spirit. The leaders have to walk a close walk with the Holy Spirit to discern what God wants of them and the people they minister. It is the Holy Spirit that teaches and opens the eyes of leaders to know deeply what areas need to grow. Fourth, church growth involves looking, observing, analyzing, quickening, and showing and pointing at the resources that God has given to the ministry. In the church there are no observers, each person is a resource for mission and ministry. Each Christian has something to contribute for the common good of the church. Fifth, church growth is local and situational, at its conception. Growth begins in Jerusalem, as Jesus said in Acts 1:8. Church growth seeks to meet the multiple needs of the local community, then, it springs forth to Judea, Samaria and to the outmost parts of the world. It is also essential to know that, church growth involves using God's Word effectively for the purposes of efficiency in cultural and social setting and context. God's word is the driver and content of church growth. Yet, the community is organized in classes, and is driven by a core value and its value system. Then church grows by meeting the needs of the people in those contexts.

A new movement is starting to influence church growth in Kenya, that is, the development of strategic plans. For example, the Anglican Church of Kenya, as a Province (ACK) has a Strategic Plan. The ACK, Dioceses of Eldoret, Kirinyaga, and Mt. Kenya South have strategic plans of growth. These plans involve SWOT philosophy of getting facts; understanding strengths and weaknesses that bring misunderstandings which hinder growth; discovery of opportunities for growth; establish priorities and set goals that are in line with principles of church growth.

Jenson and Stevens, in their book, *Dynamics of Church Growth*, introduced the notion of "balanced increase" in church growth.[3] In church growth, they posit, all things work together for the common good for all people. See Rom: 8:28-30. This balance has several components. First, quantitative growth is born out of Great Commission and Evangelism. This is the call of the church as recorded in Matthew 28:18-20 and Mark 16:15. Here membership grows and the church family gets larger. Second, qualitative growth means spiritual growth of the members. The members grow in participation in the programs of the church. The programs grow in number to include all ages and generations. For example, in an Anglican Church in Kenya, the church will grow programs that include Sunday School, Youth Service, Kenya Anglican Youth Organization (KAYO) programs, Mother's Union Programs, Kenya Anglican Men's Association (KAMA) Programs, Single Mother's Ministries, Choirs of different ages, Praise Worship Team, Widows and Widowers Ministries.

Leadership programs will include training of leaders. Third, leadership development evolves out of church growth, namely, organizational complexity. For example, All Saints Cathedral, Nairobi, has ministries beyond seven regular Sunday Services. This church has multiple worship services during the week. This church has a staff of eleven persons, focusing on various ministries. They have an administrative staff that focuses on different aspects of ministry. This kind of ministry growth shows a church that is focused on growth. Another aspect of balanced growth is physical and structural development. For example, ACK, Diocese of Thika, inaugurated in 1998, with a membership of 9,000 had a membership of 25,000 in 2009. This diocese now has a diocesan office complex, bishop's house, and has raised over Thirty Four Million Kenya Shillings (Ksh. 34Million) for over a period of ten years, 1999-2009, for developing staff

---

[3]Ron Jenson and Jim Stevens, *Dynamics of Church growth*, Grand Rapids, Michigan: Baker Book Housing Company, 1981, 10.

Defining Church Growth in the Context of Mission 13

housing, a business complex, and a hostel by Mother's Union, and a Community Empowerment and Conference Center. In this diocese, there are multiple permanent church buildings.

According to Donald MacGavran and Winfield Arn, *Ten Steps for Church Growth,* (1977), pp. 15-126, church growth must include self-governing, self-propagation, and self-supporting.[4] In other words, all Christians in a local congregation, parish, diocese, or presbytery, must be able to tell the story of their church and its ministries (propagation); support and sustain their church financially and in providing services (sustaining); and the leaders must come from their membership, (self-governing) and that they be involved in dialogue and decision-makin, hence, dialogical in its operations. In all these components, there must be unity and diversity as prescribed 1 Corinthians 12:12ff, Rom. 2: 5-8, and John 3: 3, 5. Second, all these components involve responsible membership, both formal and informal membership. In the final analysis, church growth is grounded on a personal relationship with Jesus Christ and a wholistic and holistic stewardship. Self-giving and sacrificial-giving sustains the growth of the church. In self-giving, the clergy and laity work together, giving ten percent of time and money. In sacrificial-giving, they give more and more for the ministries of the church. In doing this, they are able to pay the price of church growth.

To sustain the church, everything done must be done to the glory of God, and be Christ-Centered. Theo-centricity focuses on doing the will of God as the center for church growth. Christo-centricity focuses on growing a church which is centered on mission as intended by Christ. The problem of ego-centrism (self-centered idolatry) and ethnocentrism-monoculturalism (centered on idols of ethnicity and culture) will plague church growth. To sustain church growth, worship must remain at the center. The Christian community is sustained by worship and the study of the word of God. For example, all

---

[4]Donald A. MacGavran and Winfield C. Arn, *Ten Steps for Church Growth*, New York: Harper and Row Publishers, 1977, 5-10.

church meetings must begin with prayer and reflection on the Word of God. The Word of God sustains and nurtures the people of God. To sustain the church, the third block is intentional communication of the love of God as shown in Christ. Clergy and laity must be intentional in communicating love in all ministries. For the church to maintain the growth trend, they must know that, God demands their best, in all generations, and in all aspects of ministry. Life of "saltiness and lightness" must be lived out in holiness, righteousness and business practices.

Another issue that affects our definitions of church growth is: church growth for what and for whom. W. Paul Jones, in *Theological Worlds,*(1989), pp. 11-23, suggests that there is a crisis, "the crisis in the church today intersects the dilemma of contemporary theology ... in each mainline protestant denomination, there is a growing chasm. Liberals, on the one hand, advocate a broad relativism of options, encouraging openness as the mark of tolerance. The result in practice is often an eroding of commitment through theological indifference. The result is a Christianity that provides little more than supplemental activities and religious support for the values generally implicit in modern culture."[5] Church growth for the liberal means relativism of options that affects the lives of Christians. Church growth for the liberal also means encouraging openness and tolerance. For example, evangelism will be a crusade and presence to a gay and lesbians (homosexual). Inclusion of these homosexuals will show tolerance, at the expense of the traditionally articulated meaning of church growth. Every Biblical teaching becomes subordinated to the value of tolerance. Support services of advocacy for their civil rights and development of new liturgies for inclusion will also be seen as church growth.

On the other side, "conservative sectors have been growing in number and appeal, in part because they exhibit faith as firm com-

---

[5]W. Paul Jones, *Theological Worlds: Understanding the Alternative Rhythms of Christian Belief*, Nashville: Abingdon Press, 1989, 11.

mitment and costly discipleship, providing a cultural alternative. Yet the result in practice is often allegiance to a historically conditioned dogmatism that fails to engage the majority of persons involved in the central sectors of contemporary life."[6] To the conservative, church growth is prophecy and maintaining of *status quo*. The keeping of dogma and structures of its application is church growth. The canons of scripture and their prescriptions, once understood and applied in Christian life, lead to growth of the church, at least according to the conservative.

The functions, nature and structure of the church contribute to church growth, yet traditionalism and pluralism must give a diversified operation of the church and its members be met at their points of needs, in their contexts. This creation of alternatives will enrich the church, widen its functions, and lead to growth. Church growth of our times has to face realities of division and in-fighting that leads to conflict, separation, emptiness due to lack of meaning, judgementalism and condemnation of the different, and suffering of victims and victimizers. Church growth must work on re-uniting the Christians to healthier and mature relationships, encourage forgiveness, and living in paradox zones with courage and endurance.

Defining Church Growth in the Context of Mission

Understanding the mission of the church is paramount to defining church growth. Only when we understand the job description for the church can we be able to measure its growth, the dynamics of such growth, including hindrances to growth. The mission of the church is driven by its identity with Christ, its goals and its functions.

The mission of the church is described in 2Corinthians 5:18, as the ministry of reconciliation, and the church's role as that of being an ambassador. This ministry of reconciliation restores all persons to unity with God and with one another. The unity as a result of this reconciliation is based on identity with Christ, and for the common

---

[6]Ibid, 11-12.

good, 1Corinthians 12; 4ff. The sovereignty of God is paramount for church growth. Faithfulness, love and power of God drive the mission of the church. The work of mission in essence is God working in the world to accomplish His mission. The servant leaders who are geared and tuned to the mission of God will recognize waves, illnesses and demons in the world are use God-given resources and power to engage in mission. Using the right equipment in riding the God initiated waves, will turn the dry bones into life. God is the basic resource for mission and church growth. See 1 Corinthians 3:16.

The purposes of mission are achieved through the ministerial and pastoral functions of the church. The classical ministerial functions include: worship, prayer, preaching and proclamation, fellowship and discipleship groups, teaching, and promotion of sincere and honest life of justice, peace, and love.

The classical pastoral functions include: healing, reconciling, sustaining and guiding. The contextualized pastoral functions of the mission for the Global South include decolonization, empowering, advocacy and nurturing. This means that we are moving from Westernized ways of doing and defining mission, to seeing mission as relationally based and geared toward wholistic living. Mission for church growth is no longer a missionary oriented mission but a partnership oriented mission with the following tenets: (1) bridge-building for cross-interpretation and better understanding among the peoples; (2) cross-pollination is emphasized as people enrich each other in the context of the gospel; (3) developing dialogical relationships, where love and service are inclusive of all persons, male and female.

In bridge-building, the church in its mission must build bridges from missionary paradigms to paradigms that speak to the people in their contexts, and the needs of those communities around them. In other words, the mission must be vernacularized. One of the biggest needs for the growth and mission of the church is cross-interpretation. A Lot of assumptions are made of people, based on stereotypes. The church must lead in learning from the people and as a result take turn to interpret the people to the others.

The second most pressing issue concerns the gifts of each people and each generation. The mission of the church must emphasize that, each culture or ethnic community is needed by the other. Each culture or ethnic community is gifted for the common good. As a part of mission, the church must encourage sharing, of one with the other. One of the ways this is being accomplished is the formation of link congregations, institutions and congregations. For example, the Episcopal Diocese of Chicago, USA is linked with the Diocese of Renk, Sudan. Another example is the Diocese of Thika in Kenya which is linked with the Diocese of Exter, UK. The relationships and additional knowledge born in these linkages is enormous.

The third issue affecting church growth and its mission is the war on gender and homosexual relationships. The West has found the homosexual and transgendered communities as a mission field. African Anglican churches have found single mothers, orphaned and widowed as a mission field. Fighting abuse which is gender-based has been understood as a part of church growth and its mission. St. Paul's University, Limuru, Kenya, has a course on "Gender and Theology" and "Disability and Theology" to sensitize the clergy-to-be and practicing clergy to gender and disability issues in church and society. All these movements and outreach systems are steps toward inclusion of previously neglected communities.

Church growth and church mission must be integrated with the goal of having balance, both in bringing new members (bringing persons into a personal relationship with Christ) but also building members (bringing members into fellowship with Christ and other members). The members must also be part and parcel of growing in participation and responsible membership. Members must be empowered to a wholistic stewardship, where formal and informal aspects of membership are enhanced.

The other shift that needs to be enhanced is "the priesthood of all believers." Where Anglicans have continued to use lay persons in the midst of the Holy Orders (Deacon, Priest, and Bishop), the church has grown. A student recently reported that Presbyterians in Kenya have different ministries for the Teaching Elder and Ruling Elder. The implication is that, the mission of the church is the work of God, in action by the people of God. The Clergy and laity sense of being "called out" and being "sent out" shows an activity of both houses. We suggest here that, the corporation and collaboration between the clergy and laity in mission and ministry has positively affected the growth of the church.

The mission and growth of the church must be understood in terms of identity (being a member of the Jesus Movement) and being rooted and grounded in Christ (spiritual growth, vocation). I am writing this section after the 2007 General Elections in Kenya. The events of killing, violence and abuse that followed the contested results were done by Christians. One to one interviews revealed that Christians killed and hurt Christians. The challenge to the church included healing and reconciliation, but also redefining the mission and church growth in terms of depth in Christian transformation. Equipping, empowering, joining and serving are essential parts to church growth and the mission of the church.

Talking about church mission and growth would be amiss, if we do not mention the Great Commission as recorded in Matthew 28:19-20, Mark 16: 15-16, John 3:16 and John 20:21. Going into the world, making disciples, equipping the saints for the works of service must be an ongoing activity. The church membership will need to grow within the Pentecost Paradigm of inclusion, unity, and diversity, within herself and beyond her boundaries. Relationships among Christians, within and beyond the denominational paradigms are implicated in church growth and mission. We cannot talk about church growth and mission without acting on issues of liberation, justice, reconciliation and peace-making. It is surprising that, the Kenya Peace, Justice and Reconciliation Commission was formed without a priest in the membership. This says a lot about the place and role of the church in healing of the post-election violence in 2007 and 2008, and its aftermath. The absence of the church in the public domain during the post-election period was interpreted by some as absconding (escaping, desertion) its mission and by others as compromising with the status quo.

David J. Bosch proposes a new mission which is relevant, liberative, inclusive, mediating, acculturating and contextual.[7] We can learn from the Western mission situations, especially in America where mission has been invaded by secularization, on-going dissatisfaction on the nature of mission and ministry and feelings of a disconnected and redundant church. In a recent conversation, I was sharing the Gospel with a young man of 28 years. He reported that, he was more inclined to agnosticism because things make sense from that perspective. He discounted the church and taking a step of faith to trust in Christ, claiming that "the church is based on superstition." The challenges of African mission include neo-paganism, de-Christianization, atheism, unbelief, and pluralism. The new mission has to focus on building unity and diversity, emphasizing evangelical mission to resolve the onslaught of elitism against traditionalism, and fundamentalism.

The European and American mission has been dominated by denied racism, denial of exploiting resources of the Global South and their subjugation.

A recent occurrence affecting the war on mission, between the Anglican Liberals and Evangelicals, showed these issues are not resolved yet. The European and American Anglicans still suffer from guilt of power over their notion that they can use power-over and coercive power, as they interacted with the Global South. On the other hand, Global South Anglican leaders used reactive power under the euthanasia of shame and hence not standing to the abusive bullies of the West. The mission in this context is the use of the two love principles that stand at the core of Christianity: love of God and love of Neighbor. Genuine trust, sincere hope, a shared faith, power with and power within the community must be a part of the new mission.

---

[7]David J. Bosch, *Transforming Mission: Paradigm Shifts in Theology of Mission*, Maryknoll, New York: Orbis Books, 1991, 368-510.

In other words, mission for church growth in our times must move from: impure motives- of imperialism by use of money, theological arm-twisting, cultural demonization and ecclesiastical colonization; to pure motive- of genuine love among Christians and love of sinners to bring them to conversion, and the growth of a healthy church, and building of hope in a hopeless world. This mission will bring transformation of individuals and their communities. The emphasis for mission today must be wholistic salvation. As suggested by Bishop John V. Taylor, mission is the three-stranded presentation of the Gospel; proclamation, witnessing and service.[8] In the Kenyan context, especially in our times, we are reminded that a hungry and naked person has no ears. Hence the mission of the church is love in practice, proclamation of the Gospel by witnessing, baptizing and making disciples for Christ, and teaching-equipping, worshipping and serving. John R. Stott suggests that mission is "self-giving service which God sends His people into the world to render ... evangelism as proclaiming or announcing of the Good News of Jesus... with social action... and dialogue (for bridge building with authenticity, humility, integrity and sensitivity."[9]

In conclusion to defining church growth in the context of Mission, I must emphasize that the church will grow, with the whole membership being faithful and involved, and working toward the goal of efficiency and effectiveness in a wholistic ministry.

---

[8] Bishop John V. Taylor, *All The World*, Hodder and Stoughton, 1966, 40-43.

[9] John R. Stott, *Christian Mission in the Modern World*, Downers Grove, Illinois: InterVarsity Press, 1975, 58, 71-74.

CHAPTER THREE

Basic Assumptions of Church Growth

Introduction

The sphere of operation of a servant-leader requires one to have a theory and method that informs the practice for church growth. These are what I call basic assumptions. These are ways of thinking and acting that will define and result in church growth.

Basic Assumption One: Balanced Growth
In order to develop a balanced growth strategy for the church or to have church growth, the basic understanding is that there must be "balance." Balanced church growth alludes to the right mixture of the following variables: quantative (numbers), qualitative (spiritual growth in depth), geographical (moving outward), organizational complexity (administration and increase of groups), cultural (from monolithic to multi-ethnic, and multi-dimensional), and sociological (relational systems) growth. Balance in these seven variables will constitute a healthy congregation, parish, diocese, presbytery, or a national church.

Basic Assumption Two: Means to a Wholistic (Wholeness) and Holistic Growth
To grow a church which is sustainably growing and improving, the goal is wholistic and Holistic. A small congregation or a large national church (denomination) must work to meet persons at all multiple points of need. In that sense, there is wholeness. This same small

congregation or a large national (denomination) must also focus on righteousness, doing justice, and growing of mature Christians who love God and neighbor. The signs of such growth are: self-propagation, self-governing, and self-supporting. In self-propagation, all members participate in the programs of ministry. In self-governing, leaders are chosen from the faithful members and as servant leaders serve with the goal of encouraging and empowering the members. In self-supporting, church members are involved in self-giving and self-sacrificing for the sake of the church and its needs. Dedication, loyalty, commitment and devotion are basic tenets among the members.

Basic Assumption Three: Natural Church Growth
To grow the church takes loyalty, commitment and acting following systems of natural growth. The church will grow, if the members are in the natural growth dynamics: from birth; and to maturity. The members must be willing to pay the price of growth, that is, be willing to open new doors and take the risk of welcoming changes. The members must be willing not to engage, but disengage in personal agendas and other systems of terminal illnesses, and immune deficiency in the systems and focus on growing the church.

Basic Assumption Four: Natural Organism as a Body
The church as the "Body of Christ", must be alive, with capacity to use unity and diversity for growth, natural shock absorbers, running on effectiveness and efficiency for efficient ministry, and reaching from within and from without, and in reaching out to the needy in society. The different and diverse organs must work together of the common good.

Basic Assumption Five: Planting, Nurturing, Weeding and Harvesting
Servant leaders, both male and female must be willing to have an abundance mentality. The spirit of abundance allows all members to allow the reign of the Holy Spirit, and have a corporate and

communal renewal for the purposes of expansion. God empowering must be allowed and be seen in the life of the church.

Basic Assumption Six: Insider-Outsider Witness
A growing church will witness among its membership and outside members of the community. Members must allow themselves to be "letters to be read" to one another and within the larger community. The growing church will be in the Nave of the church and in the market places.

Basic Assumption Seven: Ministry and Vision
The ministerial and pastoral functions of the church must be Christ-Centered. The ministerial functions include preaching, teaching, worshiping and fellowship among members. The pastoral functions include healing, sustaining, guiding, reconciling, nurturing, disciplining, empowering, decolonizing and advocating. From pastoral and ministerial functions grows outreach programs and music, the basic ingredients for growth must be matured.

Basic Assumption Eight: Christian Education
While worship, music, preaching, teaching and fellowship are essential building blocks to congregational life; Christian education is the sustaining and nurturing of individuals and the community.

Basic Assumption Nine: Intentionally In Strategy and Space
The commitment to church growth must be intentional for leaders and members. This intentionality allows members to open themselves up to incomers. There is always a feeling of invasion when the church is growing. Expansion of the soul must be expected of members and their leaders. In growth, members and their leaders must use intentional strategies of growth, at a one to one level.

Basic Assumption: Faithfulness and Obedience to God are, an Essential

Christians and their leaders must understand church growth as an essential act faithfulness and obedience to God. God expects us to grow from Jerusalem (home) Judea (community), Samaria (excluded, abused and marginalized communities) and the out most parts of the world. God expects our very best in holiness, righteousness, and in the use of biblical-pastoral-clinical-protestant theology. Seeking the lost must also mean humane action, obedience to God and feeling of being found, being in the fold and on-going feeing and nurture of the individuals and the whole. Faithfulness also means renouncing rebellion and indifference and embracing restoration to normality in context.

In conclusion, we discourage leaders from being preoccupied with domestic matters and denominational of house-keeping at the expense of reaching out to a broken, conflicted, divided and wounded world. Obedience to Christ must also include renunciation of indifference and rebellion; and to restoration of normal life in the fold.

On February 26, 2006, I was talking to friends after a retreat. I had come with a message entitled: Compelled to live in the mission of God. In my reflection that night, I emphasized that a Christian must understand the world of our times to understand mission and church growth. Our world is estranged, wounded, divided, broken and at war. Our world has been taken over by globalization in terms of: politics of divide and rule; runaway capitalism, materialism and consumption; and getting rich by any means necessary, and technological advancement; and pathological narcissism of self-idolatry and monolithic cultural idolatry. This understanding informs our mission and the mission of God, and the meaning of church growth. All Christians must therefore see themselves as passionate participants, as companions, witnesses and pilgrims, prophets and hosts, and as sacraments in a world in need of servants and leaders. Therefore, the basic assumptions of church growth must be driven by a passionate and faithful response by going, proclaiming, worshipping God, making disciples and teaching, and developing of fellowship groups that incarnate the Gospel message.

A servant-leader must be committed to these basic assumptions, and be involved as a preacher, teacher, administrator, prophet, theologian, evangelist and pastor. In this book, I use the term servant-leader, connoting male or female, lay or ordained. It is important to note that, the new trends of church growth, are working within these basic assumptions, and the context must be inclusive.

Modeling for Servant Leadership

CHAPTER FOUR

Biblical and Theological Foundations of Church Growth

Introduction

In the New Testament, the word *ekklesia* is used to refer to the Christian church. *Ekklesia* is a Greek word consisting of two words: *ek* meaning 'out' and *kaleo* meaning to 'call'[1]. *Ekklesia*, which also means 'the called out' essentially means an assembly or gathering.

The term *ekklesia* was derived from a non-technical term that was used to refer to secular assemblies. It occurs 114 times in the New Testament, five of which do not refer to the New Testament church. However, it is used a hundred and nine times in a manner that is related and has connotations of the New Testament Church. Therefore, the form and meaning of the word was changed to a technical term that was then used to describe assemblies of the people of God and the Christian community as a whole. The use of the word *ekklesia* in the Gospels is also interesting (Mt 16:18 and 18:17).

In the Old Testament, the word *qahal* is used to refer to assembly, convocation, or congregation of Israel "as those belonging to the Lord" (Deut 9:10, 23:3, Judg 21:5, 8 and Mic 2:5). Ezra and Nehemiah also use this term to refer to a political body (Ezra 10:8, 12, and Neh 8:2, 17).

---

[1] http://en.wikipedia.org/wiki/Ecclesia (accessed on 12 February 2010).

In the bible, the other term used to refer to the church is *ekkleo* which also means 'the called out'. This word seems to emphasis the notion of church as people who are "elected." The origin of the call to the church is God Himself. The person who is called, is called by God (1 Cor 1:2, 11:16, 22; 2 Cor 1:1, Gal 1:13, 1 Pet. 1:2, 20, Rom 8:20, 2 Tim 1:9, 1 Thes 2:14, 2 Thes 1:4).

The Church as a Local Church

The local church is an assembly of people who profess, confess bear allegiance and faith to Jesus Christ. It is characterised by unity, uniformity, conformity and diversity. A church can mean a specific church or a group of churches (1 Thes 1:1, 1 Cor 4:17, 7:17, 2 Cor 11:8 and Gal 1:2).

Growing a church means planting and nurturing a local community of saints, who acknowledge Christ as Lord and their saviour. The church as a group meets regularly for worship (Rom 16:5). In addition, it is to be found in a particular area and at a certain time (Acts 11:22, Eph 5:32).

Church as a Universal Church

Universal church refers to a body of all believers in Christ (Mt 16:18). Here, the emphasis is on "all those constituting the Holy Catholic[2] Church." The unifying characteristic for believers is the "spiritual unity." This militant community (active on earth) is actively related to the triumphant church (church in heaven). Their fellowship epitomises their belief in Christ (Eph 1:22-23, 4:4, Acts 8:1-3, 9:31, 1 Cor 12:28, 15:9, and Col 1:18).

How does the church grow? For most people, church growth is equated to numbers. While this is not wrong, God's Word defines two types of church growth. First, there is the growth in the faith.

---

[2]The term 'Catholic' in this sense means universal. Not the Catholic Church as we know it today to refer to the Roman Catholic Church led by the Pope.

Numbers may stand still, and yet a church can grow considerably over the years. That is, they grow in 'faith'. God desires this very much. In fact, this was the first and foremost reason Christ planted His church (Jn 6:29). Therefore, growing this church is growing "the belief in Christ". This growth is seen from the past, present and the future (Eph 1:22, and Heb 12:23).

Of course, the second kind of church growth is about numbers. God's Word says that He desires all to come to the knowledge of salvation (1Tim 2:3-4). So, He gave the church the great commission to go and make disciples (Mt 28:19-20). Therefore, God desires is that His church grows in numbers. The Great Commission in Matthew speaks and instructs us to make disciples by baptizing and teaching, and source or reach them from all nations of the world. God tells us that, He grows the church, through His Word and Sacraments of Baptism and Holy Communion ; and teaching, says Paul, which includes preaching (Eph 4:11).

Contemporary Uses of the Term Church

In the contemporary world, the term church has acquired several meanings. Some of them are outlined below:

1. A building in which Christians meet for worship.
2. A religious service conducted by Christians.
3. Anglicans use the term to refer to an organisation of churches in a province[3].
4. A denomination with the same doctrine.

The church as a denomination is composed of believers who are bound by the Christian doctrine. They are all united by worship, preaching, instruction, fellowship and service to God and humanty.

---

[3] http://en.wikipedia.org/wiki/Anglicanism (accessed 19 February 2009).

The Church as an Organism

An organism is an animal or plant, especially one that is so small that you cannot see it without using a microscope. The Church as the body of Christ can be viewed as is an organism. It is vitally connected with the Head of the body and receives its sustenance, guidance and direction from the Head (Eph 4: 15-16). At the beginning, the Church had no human head on earth, such as Moses. The role of the apostles was only to preach the sole authority of the Lord Jesus. Where there conflicts such as circumcision of Gentiles, they were settled by the word of God (Acts 15: 7-8; 17-18).

The church can therefore be looked at as a living organism[4] because of the following seven factors:

1. The church is alive (Rev 3:1ff, 1 Cor 12:12ff and Rom 12:1ff).
2. The church grows (Mt 13:31, 17:20 and Lk 13:19).
3. The church has radiance, righteousness and holiness (Eph 5:27, Mk 7:6, 16:15, Mt 26:58 and Acts 11:26).
4. The church has order (Eph 4:11, Mt 5:14 and 1 Cor. 14:40).
5. The church is a natural system, with natural growth tendencies, such as unity, diversity, differentiation and expansion (Acts 1:8).
6. The church is always giving 'birth' by bringing sinners into the faith (Mt 5:27-28, 44:22:37).
7. The church is always bearing good fruit (Mt 7: 17-20).

The Church and its Metaphors

Metaphors are images that bring life to the meaning of a word. It is a creative way of describing something by referring to something else which is the same in a particular way. For example, if you want to say that someone is very brave and courageous, you can say that the person is a lion. Several metaphors are used in the bible to refer to the church. Some of them are as follows:

---

[4] http://www.biblecentre.org/topics lmg_topics_is_the_church_an_organization.htm.

1. The church is the body of Christ (Col 1:9-18, 24; Eph 1:16-23, 5:29-30, and 1 Cor 12:27).
2. The church is the branches (John 15:1-8).
3. The church is the bride of Christ (2 Cor 11:2-3, Rom 7:2-4, Eph 23-30, and Rev 19:7-8, 21:2).
4. The church is the temple (1 Cor 3:16, 2 Cor 6:16, Eph 2:19-22, Heb 3:6, 1 Pet 2:4-7, Mt 16:18.

Metaphors for the Believers

Just is as is the case with the church, many metaphors are used to refer to believers. Some of them are as follows:
1. The chosen race and a royal priesthood (1 Pet 2:9).
2. Believers (Acts 4:32; 5:14, 1 Tim 4:12, Jn 14:6).
3. Brothers or sisters (Rom 8:9-17, 29, Acts 15:36).
4. Saints that are set apart (Acts 9: 13, 32; 1 Cor 1:2 and Eph 5: 22-27).
5. The elect or chosen ones (1 Pet 1:1-24, Col 3:12-14).
6. Disciples or learners (Acts 6:1-7, Eph 2:1-22, and Mt 28:16-20.
7. Christians (Acts 11:26, Gal 2:20).
8. Those of the way (Acts 9:2, 22:4; 24:14, 22 and Jn 14:6).
9. The sheep (Jn 10:3, 7 and 21:17).
10. A fellowship (1 Cor 1:9, 5:2, 2 Cor 6:14, and 1 Jn 1:6, 7. Believers are also called soldiers 2 Tim 2:3. Believers are also called servants (Rom 6:18, Col 1:23, Lk 17:10 and Jn 12:26).
11. Friends (Jn 15:15-16).

12. See also http://www.nairobichapel.org/Pages/ekklesia.asp (accessed on 12 February 2010) and http://www.allaboutgod.com/christian-doctrine.htm for further understanding of the usage of the term, "church."

Contextual Factors affecting Church Growth from a Biblical Perspective

The convenient location of the church and its visibility is implied by St. Paul's starting of local congregations. The church in that sense is also placed in the market place and it becomes the centre of community life in that locality. These two factors contributes to its growth. The spiritual activities and a sense of ownership by the community, both the community in the church and that community that surround it contribute to its growth. St. Andrew's Episcopal Church, Evanston, Illinois, USA was almost closed down for loosing its former glory of being the centre of community life. The program of growth, as initiated under my tenure aimed at re-packaging the church as a centre of community activities. We began a music school for the community. We initiated a summer program for youth in the community. We provided pastoral counselling and psychotherapy services for the community. I became a pastor of the community, and was involved in community issues. In Kenya, churches were known for starting schools, medical clinics, and hospitals as ways of reaching out to the community. A new trend is starting in Kenya, where most denominations are starting universities and conference facilities.

The church as always had the open door policy. This showed hospitality and care for the needs of community. The Episcopal Church Relief Fund and the Episcopal Development Fund have been avenues of Anglicans in the USA to reach out to the needy communities. It hurts the communities, both the giving and receiving when these ministries to the poor and needy are politicized or used a systems of settling theological scores. In Kenya, the churches joined hands to serve the Internally displaced persons after the post-election violence of January 2008. This visibility and activities in the communities contribute to church growth. The church must be where the community is and meet the community at its points of need. In the ACK, Diocese of Thika, the church collected food for the dying hungry during the drought of 2008 and 2009. In other words, a growing church is not only open and used on Sunday, for two hours only. The church must remain open during the week for various community activities.

The New Testament Church is also seen to have conducted worship with simplicity, and studying God's word diligently. The music we have inherited from the West is communication of God's word, in simple ways and within their cultural expressions, thus speaking to the souls of the people. In 2009, I was privileged to visit the Anglican Diocese of Exter, UK and as their celebrations of the 110th anniversary of ministry. The regular and traditional church was changed to feel like a theatre, with the goal of meeting the young people in the "hip-hop" culture. These young people felt included and welcome. The people of the town gathered one night for an orchestra concert, with secular and sacred music. A growing church as we are shown by the apostle Paul must be seen and experienced as inclusive. Yet the church must be light, salt and yeast in the world. The church must have distinctions and clarity to call sin, sin, and not call what is not sin to be sin.

A reader of the Pauline Epistles will see a growing church which was Christ-Centred, yet the local Christian community owned and served it with devotion and dedication. A growing church must have members who feel God has called them together with a purpose and He has called them to responsibility and accountability. A growing and mature church does not have "observing Members", rather all members are involved meeting their own needs and those outside, to a point that it becomes a sending church.

A reader of the Pastoral Letters of Paul will see a church engaged in equipping, discipling, empowering and grounding people. Paul also shows a church that was challenged by individualized agendas, personality conflicts and financial difficulties. The "common good" was a more serious agenda, as service and gifts for ministry became the centre piece.

The Early Church as shown in its growth in the Acts of the Apostles moved from being a Hebrew-Centred mission to a Samaritan-Roman-Centred mission. We can learn from here that native, ethnic, and cultural mentalities have their place in the incarnation and living out the Gospel in practice. Yet a growing church cannot afford to go native, when it is over-identified or fused to the idols and negativities of ethnocentrism and monoculturalism. For example, the church in Kenya uses a harambee system to support its mission financially. This harambee system has been used by the church. Politicians who are invted as "Guests of Honor" have used this Harambee Syetm as a forum of propagating negative ethnicity, exclusion and division. The funeral and burial ceremonies are sacred moments that have also been some of the best moments of caring for bereaving families and community. For all intentions and purposes, these ceremonies have been *kairos* moments of growing the church, yet these burial rites have become forums for political agenda and fighting. The Kenyan growing church has to define itself by having purpose and intentions of growing within certain boundaries. Meaning that, weedings, funerals and Harambee must be used for mission.

The early Church as shown by the Apostle Paul was besieged by individual problems as personalities wanted to be the centre of interests. Personality-driven churches grow as long as that person is alive, and at times, the personal becomes a hindrance to church growth. A growing church must work against negative basic assumptions as demonic forces. These include: complaining, burnout, fighting, flight, refusal to take responsibility for ones own actions, blaming and condescending attitude, development of illegal leaders, moral problems of sexual abuse and infidelity, financial mismanagement, personalization and privatization of ministry affairs, and demanding privileges and prestige by splitting off and cold war in-fighting. When there is delegation, it must be delegation of activity and not accountability, thus assuring that, those who delegate are still held accountable for the work done on their behalf.

In conclusion, the church must be the church, and must be grown using biblical and theological resources to define its mission objectives and develop a firm foundation for growth.

Church Mission

The mission of the church is defined in its ministry. The ministry of the church begins with the Great Commission. In examining Mark 16: 15-16, Matthew 28:19-20, John 20:21 and John 3:16, there is a clear sense that, we cannot speak of church growth without understanding the mission. The work of going into the world, making disciples, teaching and training them in the truth is a part of the bulk of the multi-dimensional mission work. We cannot speak of church growth without looking at the basic foundation of church growth, which is, faith in Christ. Our love for Christ, loyalty and a commitment of being a Christian is a requirement for church growth. Think of the common foundation will protect church leaders and all Christians for the two common errors. First, Christians must be against being too ego-centric and proud of their abilities and gifts. We all must be clear that these gifts, talents, and abilities are intended for the common good. Second, all Christians must work against the sin of being observer and as persons with nothing to offer. Every Christian has something to offer to the ministries of the church. In 1 Corinthians 12: 4ff, there is a gift of diversity and not of difference. Diversity in gifts (see Galatians 3:26-29) suggests clearly that each has been given, individual identities are a part and parcel of what God intended in the church, for the purposes of growth. The variety includes wisdom, knowledge, faith, healing, miracles, prophesy, discernment of spirits, various kinds of tongues, and interpretation of tongues.

The mission of the church must be understood in terms of the ministry as shown and recorded in 2 Corinthians 5: 18. The ministry of reconciliation is to restore all persons to unity with God, and into unity with one another. This ministry is only possible, in the Name, and ministry of Christ Himself.

Mission is also articulated in terms of: identity (faith in Christ and being grounded in Christ), purpose (of reconciliation), ministerial functions (worship, preaching, fellowship, discipling and teaching, reaching out to the needy in community), and promotion of sincere and honest life of justice, peace and love among all people; and in terms of pastoral functions (healing, reconciliation, guiding, sustaining, prophesying, faithing, discipling, liberating, empowering and decolonizing).

Mission is also the work of God in action, where God meets people at their points of need. See Luke 9. 1-2. With a sense of God sending, then identity and vocation are an integral part to mission. See Exodus 3:10, and John 20:21. When we are speaking of church growth, we are speaking in terms of the on-going work of the Holy Spirit as a Pentecost experience. See Acts 2: 1-12, 42-48.

Titus Presler in *Horizons of Missions* suggests a composite list of ten aspects of church growth.[5] These include: preaching the Gospel; service as sacraments; live as companions; be pilgrims; nurture all dimensions of humanness; struggle for justice, peace, and reconciliation; be partners with collaboration; express the Gospel in diversity of culture; cooperate with persons of other faiths, and celebrate as a Eucharistic community.

In conclusion of this chapter, I must emphasize that, identity in Christ informs ministerial and pastoral functions. Call in Christ automatically translates to loyalty, comittment, and being "sent-out-ones" and the activity of incarnating Christ in mission and ministry.

---

[5]Titus Presler, *Horizons of Mission*, 155-177.

CHAPTER FIVE

The Church as a System and Its Models

Introduction

Von Bertalanffy defines a system as "a set of elements standing in an interaction."¹ It is characterised by parts that combine to form a whole. For the whole to function, all the parts work simultaneously in line with a fixed plan or set of rules. Nevertheless, each part is different and has its own characteristics and functions. Therefore, the whole is not necessarily the sum of its parts.

Dynamics of the Church as a System

In this chapter, I want to emphasize that church growth must be influenced by understanding the systems within the church. Edwin H. Freedman in his ground breaking book, *Generation to Generation: Family Process in Church and Synagogue*, (1985) introduced my thinking of the church as a system. I once preached in a church where the baptism and Holy Communion services were run concurrently. I will use this example to show the dynamics of a church system. The church as a system has five dynamics: mechanical, physiological, circulatory, psychological, social or philosophical systems.

---

¹Ludwig von Bertalanffy, *General Systems Theory: Essays on Its Foundation and Development*, New York: George Braziller, 1969.

First, the church is a mechanical system. During the service I have referred to above, the archdeacons – two male clergy were assisted at the altar by two women leaders. In the nave of the church, there were ushers and elders who were distributing bulletins, hymn books and prayer books to the congregation. At the keyboard, there was an organist with two assistants. The congregation was invited to take the offerings and tithe pledges to the front. One of the church members later observed, in a conversation with me that, everything had worked together well, except that he saw a warden take money from the collection plate. Therefore, as a mechanical system the church has parts which perform different functions to make the work of worship complete. Dysfunctions or a dysfucntion muat be understood as a systems problems. The warden who took money upon pouring it on the table was a system's problem. Checks and balances in the systems operation were organized in a way that, two people must be present at the table before money is poured our from the collection box. The system was changed to fit with other sub-systems.

Second, as a physiological system, the church has several systems within 'its body'. For example, an announcement was made in church that the archdeacon had met with the whole council of the church, comprising of clergy and lay persons. This meeting had made a crucial decision: the altar was to be completed before the visit by the bishop. Thus, the Mother's Union, Kenya Anglican Men's Association (KAMA), the Kenya Anglican Youth Organisation (KAYO) and group leaders were asked to propose a main guest. Here, we see the interaction of the church system and its sub-systems like the church council, Mother's Union and the Youth Organisation in a physiological way.

Third, the church as a psychological system has intellectual and emotional sub-systems that guide the behaviour of its members. These sub-systems are bridged by a feeling system.[2] Maturity of

---

[2] Bowen Murray, *Family Therapy in Clinical Practice,* Northvale, New Jersey: Jason Aronson, 1978.

this psychological system is portrayed by unity, diversity and the capacity to play different roles without causing anxiety. Closed, highly open or diffused psychological systems negatively affect interpersonal and institutional relationships and can have dire consequences. Closed systems have tight boundaries that do not allow interaction with those outside. Closed systems are negatively clanish and ethnocentric. Highly open systems have no boundaries or differeentiation of roles. Every one becomes a jack of all trade and a master of none. Diffused systems have unclear and confused boundaries in the system. What is needed in the system is a balance in the system, allowing flexible boundaries. These boundaries are clearly known, and yet can be made flexible to meet challenges of circumstances.

Fourth, the church as a social system is an organisation. It gives roles, functions, rights and privileges to benefit or satisfy social needs. The system is relational (the church is a relational community) and dialogical (the church is a communication system, within itself and with God as a veritcal conversation)

Fifth, the church as a spiritual system endeavours to meet members' expectations. We have to remember that each member has motivations, needs and longings. The church meets people at their points of need as it incarnates the love of God. The church is a transforming and liberating community.

The Church as an Organisation

The church as a philosophical and theological system is an organised institution. All churches have sets of presuppositions, core values, a value system, methods, techniques, principles, doctrines and beliefs that members adhere to. These philosophical guidelines explain the meaning, purpose and direction of life to members. There are five disciple-making blocks for purposeful church growth[3]: single-minded direction (seeing clearly together as a congregation); deep-seated

---

[3] Jensen and Stevens, *Dynamics of Church Growth*, 1981, 51. New York: The Guilford Press, 195-309.

desire (wanting growth in ministry passionately); God-vision and God-given strength for accomplishing (Spirited enthusiasm); step by step faithfulness for action (bulldogged tenacity); and regular evaluations (assessment, review, realignment and rededication for mission in context). These five dynamics are basic blocks to our understanding the church, parish or diocese as a family system which is committed to growth.

The systems perspective sees growth or hindrance to growth to be embedded in the system as a whole. A person who uses energy to focus on mission or defocus in mission does that on behalf of the whole congregation, parish or diocese. The systems' perspective uses the following categories to understand the church as a system:

Identified Patient

Identified patient is a term used in a clinical setting to describe the person in a dysfunctional family who has been subconsciously selected to act out the family's inner conflicts in order to keep attention focused on him or her, as an element that lies outside of the core conflict. The identified patient may display unexplainable emotional or physical symptoms, and is often the first person to seek help, often at the bequest of the family. As the family focuses on this person, it forgets that, the problem is in the system.

Just like in the clinical setting, the church also has an identified patient, who is a scapegoat and carrier of the problems of the church, parish or diocesan system. The idea of the identified patient in the congregation, parish or diocese shows that, we do focus on the individual in the church who is a problem, fighting, complaining, burned out, hyperactive, or excessive in his or her behaviour. But, rather, I am suggesting that, he/she is an extension of the problems in the church, parish or diocese as a whole. The idea here is that: the church has an identified patient who carries the stress or pathology of the system, in the congregation. The pathology of a dysfunctional parish, diocese or congregation is showing up in that individual, yet the problem is in the diocese. This means that, the whole church is the unit of the treatment to heal this individual and the diocese is the unit of treatment. The focus must be on the relational systems in the congregation, parish or diocese.

Trying to isolate this person as the "sick one" is to misdirect the relational systems of the whole. To isolate an individual and see him or her as a source of ineffectiveness and inefficiency in a congregation, parish or diocese is not the right way of seeing from a systems perspective. The creation of an identified patient is an unconscious process, done by projection (throwing to) and introjections (taking in) and behaving as projected. This person is only a bearer of the strength or the sickness of the system. This person's over-functioning or under-functioning, dysfunctioning, super-positive, super-negative is a promotion of the problems in the congregation, parish, diocese or presbytery. Each family member has a position and its roles and activities are what maintain the ministries of the whole. From this systems perspective, each person contributes and is involved in the emotional system, to benefit all and contribute to the growth of the entire system.

Homeostasis (Balance)
The concept of *homeostasis* is grounded on the tendency for people in relationship to strive for relational balance. This tendency for balance is sought in self-regulating ways, and self-corrective ways and with the goal of self-preservation. This is a natural order, that everything done in a family system is geared toward this balance and maintenance of identity. This balance assures relational continuity and congruency, as well as role taking, and decision-making with ease and comfort. When there is imbalance, which is what I call "relational pathology" in the system, people experience anxiety. In terms of the structural organization, each person in the system has a position, resources, authority and power to maintain the balance of the whole system. Anxiety distablizes the fucntioning of the system.

A dysfunctional church is a church in which conflict, misbehaviour, sexual misconduct, unethical fuctioning and abuse on the part of individual members of the church occur continually and regularly, leading other members to accommodate such actions. The church is a "spiritual home" for its members. For me, and my family, we have lived and travelled around Kenya, and abroad, but our church, ACK, St. John's, Gakoe is always home, a place that we can return and enjoy being there for worship, fellowship, relationships, belonging and participating. The Agikuyu say: East or West, Home is best. As a home, the church must also have a sense of balance *(homeostasis)*. When there is a malfunction, there are mechanisms within the church that help naturally in transforming and resolving conflicts. Each person keeps to his role and its functions. It is always difficult to change church officers and their positions; hence there is resistance to change of the organization structure or the individuals holding offices. The members are interdependent in their functioning. Each is independent in that, each person comes to church with individualized personal needs and longing. This is called paralled-interdependence in the church, parish or diocese, as each is connected to God, the main source of life, yet each goes to God directly. On the other hand, Christians in a church, congregation or diocese or presbytery are related and connected to one another as a body, each runs through the other. This is called serialed-interdependence. Edwin H. Friedman argues that, a congregation has an emotional system, organisational structure, trans-generational transmission, functional parts, reality, and positions in the system.[4]

Differentiation of Self in the System
The idea of differentiation has to do with the capacity for self awareness. There is a boundary between "I" and "We" in being an individual self, and yet there is a communal self. Meaning that, each family member is different from the other. Each has gifts, talents, graces and deficits, weaknesses and growing edges. Each person has personal goals and values, yet there are communal goals and values. There is "togetherness" and "separateness" among the family

---

[4] Edwin H. Friedman, *Generation to Generation: Family Process in Church and Synagogue*, New York: The Guilford Press, 195-309.

members. Each individual has his or her own line of development, just as the family has its own line of development. There are also shared values of ethnic and cultural community. Each person has to take personal and communal responsibilities and accountabilities. There are personal and communal destinies.

The church has a *homeostasis*, or a balance; the church members must have self differentiation. The idea of *homeostasis* suggests that, the church members have relationships, between themselves and with God. Naturally as new beings, in Christ, they self-correct themselves in living to self-preserve, self-propagate, and self-support. This means that, the church organises herself in dynamic ways to serve her common good. There are four dysfunctional dynamics that attack differentiation. The first one is the dynamic of disengagement done by an individual, congregation, or diocese, or presbytery. This is where one member, church, or diocese or presbytery become a "loner." This involves excluding of others in the name of "self-reliance" and "independence." A church member who disengages others, and takes actions alone must be challenged to engage the community. The second dysfunction is one "stuckness." Here a person is not allowed voice, and is forced to sacrifice for the sake of other. This system is abusive of individual rights, privileges and accountabilities. Church members who have held office for too long should be allowed to retire or step down for the sake of training others. The third dysfunction is one of "sabotage and seduction." In this dysfunction, the individual experiences coercion whenever he or she seeks to grow in differentiation. Coercion into the ministries of the church through back-door tactics should be discouraged by all means. The fourth dysfunctional dynamic is one of "showering with gifts, praise and quick adoration." This involves maintaining and containing of the pathological anxiety by keeping the status quo, by showering blessings like gifts, praise and quick adoration (peddle-stalling). Church leaders should not be praised as a system of covering needs for change. These four dynamics do not lead to church growth. Rather, they hinder church growth and encourge dysfunctional systems.

Extended Kinship Dynamics

The African mind-set about family dynamics and the inter-generation connections in terms of the kinship systems and the living-dead, and their influences to our daily life is common knowledge. The nuclear family comprises of parents and siblings. The extended family includes other fathers, mothers, sisters and brothers, and the multiple grandparents. The kinship system includes uncles, aunts, cousins, and other distant relatives. The systems theory as presented here suggests that, patterns of behaviour, thinking, perceiving and behaving, and systems of dealing with emotional problems are transmitted from generation to generation. Issues such as sex, money, kinship land possession, burial rites, drinking of alcohol, attachment and separation, marital relationships, and physical health are handled the same way from generation to generation. These inter-generational transmissions aid or hinder relationships and functioning systems. More specifically, they can aid or hinder differentiation and growth. To grow up, one maintains the emotional connections with the family of origin and the extended family. There is a necessity of differentiation from this functional system. The parameters of differentiation are involved in matters of faith, responsibility and accountability, and relationships in the faith community, the church. Just as the issues of relationships, thinking, behaving, and staying connected are important in marital relationships, they are important in church. Hence our families of origin and extended families are a part of the grounding and being in church. If trust was low in the family of origin and the extended family, the same will happen in church. Churches grow or hindered from growth by tradition, personality, finances, programs, building projects, events, seekers-orientation. Where as mature churches must have all these aspects to serve a multi-generation community, if overly driven by any of these aspects, growth will be hindered in the spiritual community.

The church as a system has a structure just like a family and it must manage its affairs within boundaries of differentiation. The church as discussed in chapter one to four has multi-generational transmissions of strategies, emotional processes, and natural systems of healing and correcting itself, given time and space.

Emotional Triangles
An emotional triangle is formed with three person operations, or when three persons are involved with an issue. The main concept of triangles is that, when two persons become uncomfortable with each other, over an issue or over an emotional process, they involve a third person or a third issue, as a way of stabilizing or bringing pathological *homeostasis* in their relationship or as a way of dealing with the issue.

The church has dynamics of the nuclear family and the extended family; and the church has emotional triangles. For example, a vicar had a problem with his curate or assistant. Instead of dealing directly with their problem, they brought in a Choirmaster to be part of the solution. In another case, a viar had a problem with the Choirmaster, intead of releasing him from his job, he brought the church committee to deal with him.

In other words, the church has observable interactions, communication systems, channels of delivering ministerial and pastoral functions, and authority systems. To introduce changes in the system, the members and their pastor(s) engage in discussions to avoid fighting, running away or the increase of un-serious leaders.

The pastor uses inter-generational theological tools in the situations, and within God's purpose and will to reach wholistic and holistic ends of the parish or parishioner. Also to maintain balance, there must be differentiation against "too much togetherness or stuckness" (serial relationships) or "too distant, emotional cut-off, great distant or rugged individualism (parallel relationships). The balance is that of interdependence. The comfort of members is found in awareness of one's needs and longings in the midst of a congregational life.

The 'I-We' balance, allows one to live and practice faith personally and yet connected, belonging and participating in congregational and community life. If there is no differentiation and balance, the result is anxiety, conflict and fighting, running away and burnout, and spiritual depression.

The Message of Trinity
The Church is Trinitarian, a community born of God, the Father, Son and Holy Spirit. The church stays healthy when it allows the activities of the One God in three persons to work among her membership. There are balanced emotions loaded and apprehended in these relationships with each of this One in Three persons.

If one is related to two of the three persons, there is anxiety and discomfort, and emotions and focus are on the third person. In a congregation, "the most pervasive triangles are ... the clergy person and an individual's personal salvation, or the clergy's own personal family and the congregational family.[5]

Conclusion

There are strong emotional conflicts and triangles, as people focus on the processes triggered. The church, congregation, diocese or presbytery will grow when the leader learns and uses these five dynamics and their effects in the ministry and mission of the church.

The above mentioned five dynamics of a system can also be used as the congregation, parish, diocese, or presbytery think and act on their images. The familiar images I see or have seen include evangelist, survivor, prophetic, pillar, pilgrim, liberator, servant and leader.

---

[5]*Ibid.*, 36

CHAPTER SIX

Models of Church Growth: Jesus and Paul

Introduction

The two basic models of church growth presented in this chapter are found in the New Testament. These are Jesus' and Paul's Models. The Chapter shows how both can work to make the church grow. Jesus' model begins with the Great Commission (Mt 28:19-2o (also Mk 16:15) and grows into the unrestrained heart (Acts 1:8b). We see Jesus' disciples embark on missions to many nations, baptising and converting followers, following the stoning of Stephen and the following period of persecution. See Acts 5:42, and 11:19-20. The growth and spread of the church includes going into Jerusalem, Judea, Samaria, and many parts of the earth.

Contrary, Paul's model grows from a personal encounter with Christ that leads to preaching and defending the Gospel to his own people, the Hebrews. It later moves to a cross-cultural crusade whereby he preaches to Gentiles. He later on makes many missionary journeys preaching the word whose final result is formation of an organised church. To have a clear idea of how the church grows and possible hindrances to church growth, we need to read about Paul from his conversion, how he defends his conversion, his missionary journeys, and finally the Pastoral Letters he writes.

Jesus' Model of Church Growth

The Great Commission begins when Jesus commissions His disciples and gives them authority to go and preach the message of salvation (Mk 16:16; Mt 28:16-20). He tells them to go and make disciples of all nations, baptising them in the Name of the Father and of the Son and of the Holy Spirit, and to teach them to obey everything that He has commanded them. Therefore, the dynamics of Church growth require the evangelist and preacher to be commissioned by Christ. Christ's authority is central to His ministry and to the ministry of disciples (Mk 1:27 and Lk 8:25). Commissioning by the sending agency makes the messenger an agent. Members of the Anglican Church of Kenya are commissioned by the bishop during their confirmation.[1]

This model involves going, making, baptising, teaching and obedience. These five aspects of the process are seen in Jesus' ministry. So He says, "As the Father has sent me, so send I send you" (Jn 20:21). They are sent to "all nations" (Mk 13:10).

This model is also expounded on by Jesus when He tells his disciples, "But you will receive power when the Holy Spirit comes on you; and you will be my witnesses in Jerusalem, and in all Judea and Samaria and to the ends of the earth" (Acts 1:8b). The first thing that we notice here is the Gift of the Holy Spirit which is given as spiritual equipment for a worldwide campaign. God keeps His promise and we see the birth of the church after the disciples experience the Holy Spirit (Acts 2:2; 2:38). Missionary campaigns, crusades and open air meetings where the Gospel is preached are driven and empowered by God. All Christians are therefore called upon to recognise their role as instruments of the Holy Spirit. The scope and width of the missionary area is Jerusalem (to self, in the homes and local area). The congregation's local community and immediate surrounding area is Judea. The surrounding districts and

---

[1] "Confirmation and Commission Service," *Anglican Church of Kenya, Book of Common Prayer*, Nairobi: Uzima Press, 2002, 2003, 57-63.

provinces, the unloved and unwanted in society is Samaria. Finally, the ends of the Earth are world mission, other countries and continents.

Jesus' model suggests increase in numbers and in geographical area. It also suggests qualitative increase where Christians learn to love the Lord and love one another. They also learn to give service to God and to one another. Church growth here also means relationships among the communities of Christians. Since they are filled with the Holy Spirit, Christians, as individuals and as Christian communities must grow physically, mentally, spiritually, and socially. The church grows not only in unity and conformity, but also in diversity. In this model, the church is required to be selfless. Peter was commissioned to this notion of a self-giving and self-sacrificing church. He was re-commissioned and challenged to love, serve and feed the hungry (Jn 21:15).

Paul's Model of Church Growth

Paul's model of Church growth has six main aspects as discussed below. The first aspect is based on the messenger being transformed by the message. Paul's personal encounter with Christ meant everything to him. His commissioning is also important. He is told not just to preach to the House of Israel but also to the Gentiles. It grows from one ethnic community, to a cross-cultural community; and to an international Christian community. Paul's preaching to Jews and Gentiles remained a core aspect of the missionary journeys.

The second aspect is that of bringing believers to a convenient place, either in a home or in a public location. A growing church is a worshipping and fellowshipping community that meets regularly.

The third aspect is that of believers meeting in groups. Believers met regularly for worship, fellowship, and instruction in Christian doctrine and conduct. These first congregations had to learn the meaning and purpose of Christian experience. They had to learn the meaning of conversion and justification by faith and its practice in daily life. They needed each other for encouragement as they fought against persecution, backsliding, worldly things and the devil's temptations. The excitement in the new life under Christ brings joy and new energy for life. In the first phase of Christian experience, the battles are fierce, hence the need to meet and encourage one another.

The fourth aspect for Apostle Paul was the development of servant leaders. The art and science of making leaders as Paul shows us takes a lot of hard work. For Paul, servant-leaders, elders and deacons were chosen from among the local Christian people. The goal of servant leadership is to live by example, and develop a balanced church which is stable and mature to support itself, reach out to its communities and beyond.

The fifth aspect is that of reaching out to the neighbours – across ethnic and cross political boundaries. This required Paul to have a strategic plan for the neighbouring communities. This is an example of a church expanding.

The sixth aspect and facet for Paul was that of a mature church. He understood church maturity to mean having programmes for all, an all inclusive church; and a self-supporting, self-governing, and self-propagating church. A mature church not only meets its own needs, but also supports mission in other areas, including abroad. The mature church is described by Paul in Ephesians (Eph 4:11-16).

The Church Life Cycle

The Church Life Cycle refers to its birth, growth, maturity, decline, near death experiences, and rebirth. Two cases as outlined below show that maturity can turn into immaturity, but a change can occur to rebirth maturity. Lyle Schaller in his book, *Activating a Passive Church* suggests that naming a church, knowing its personality in terms of complex realities strength and liabilities can help leaders to diagnose and develop a treatment program from the internal dynamics.[2] St. Andrew's Episcopal Church in Evanston, Illinois,

---

[2]Lyle Schaller, *Activating a Passive Church*, Nashville: Abingdon Press, 1981, 10-15.

USA, was begun by the African American community, at the height of fighting for their rights. Having been forced to worship very early, before their masters at St. Mark's Episcopal Church, Evanston, Illinois, USA, the members, all Black, built this church with a lot of passion. It became the centre of their lives and a centre of community life. These people not only worship there, but the also organized for their civil rights in the country. It was a mature congregation with inter-generational ministries, know in the whole town. For over ten years, this church had poor lay and clergy leadership. By the time I got there in June of 1993, the church was experiencing near death stage. For a period of three years, we held discussions and planned for re-birth. Thirteen years later, we all had given the church a second chance by giving a re-birth of its ministries. Mary Sellon, Daniel Smith and Gail Grossman in their book, *Redeveloping the Congregation* suggest that, forming a core team, birthing and welcoming a vision of mission and ministry, owning and being owned by that vision, empowering and removing of barriers are the anchors for change and growth.[3] For many churches in Kenya, they are still in the birth stages. Some are being reborn after being inherited from being colonial chaplaincies. For example, St. Christopher's, Nakuru Town in the diocese of Nakuru, and Thika Memorial Church in the diocese of Thika. These churches are in their first generation of leadership and ministries. They have become vibrant, and are serving with communities with passion and new energies.

The Apostle Paul shows that maturity requires the development of unity and diversity as leaders prepare and equip the saints for the work of service (Eph 4:11-12). This out-wards looking church, from an inward increase among its members and development of capabilities among them brings maturity. The church that grows

---

[3] Mary K. Sellon, Daniel P. Smith, and Gail F. Grossman, *Redeveloping the Congregation*, New York: The Alban Institute, 2002.

allows diversity and has an appreciation of the many gifts brought into the church.

A growing church grows in its Christ-Likeness, in behaviour and character. Paul has listed the characteristics of growth as: unity, love, stability, and capacity to adapt (Eph 4:13-15). Maturity of the church in this sense is perfection and being grounded in Christ, both for individual Christians and their community. A growing church is a church of genuine love and life in Christ.

The growing church as the community of the King must discover itself: within the cosmetic dimension of the personal knowledge of Christ; a recovery of the dynamic breadth of the Scripture; a recovery of its sense of historicity; stressing the ethics of the Kingdom, and the rediscovery of the multi- cultural mandate.[4] The model of church growth must reflect the Christ-like images. It must not be like the models of a lecture theatre, movie theatre, a corporation or a social club. Avery Dulles gives better models of church as the ideal community: the church as an institution, as a mystical communion, as a sacrament, as a herald, and as a servant.[5] For Paul the church is an agent, called, sent, and acting. That means that a growing church should involve its members in its programmes as essential parts of the whole (Eph 4:16).

Conclusion

For the church in Kenya to grow, it can borrow from, both Paul's and Jesus' model of church growth. One important aspect is having a convenient place for believers to meet. The church should then be a visible and active church. It can even be a church at the market place so long as there is worship, fellowship, preaching, teaching and musical-movement. It should genuinely reach out to and attract followers irrespective of age, race colour or ethnic community.

---

[4]Howard A. Snyder, *The Community of the King*, Downers Grove, Illinois: InterVarsity Press, 1977, 29-30.

[5]Avery Dulles, *Models of Church*, New York: Image Books, Doubleday, 1974, 1987, 34-102.

The churches in Kenya have the challenge of remaining in their imperative, to establish the Kingdom of God which will bring about living in real *"shalom"*, peace among Kenyans, especially after the 2007 disputed elections that saw the country torn on ethnic lines. The Gospel responsibility of proclamation of the Kingdom of God must also embrace the social responsibility, of meetings persons beyond spiritual needs. Jesus' and Paul's models as discussed above show the need for a relevant, comprehensive and wholistic preaching. Conversion of the soul is essential, but preaching of justice, and service and advocacy for the poor, exploited, abused, excluded and marginalized are equally important. From these two models, we learn that the church must engage in a comprehensive engagement of mission.

Modeling for Servant Leadership

CHAPTER SEVEN

Leadership Positions and Mission for Growth

Introduction

The mission of the church is defined and understood in terms of the ministry of reconciliation (2 Cor 5:18). Our reconciliation with God is the basic foundation. The next level is reconciliation with one another, and is meaningfully lived out in love. The mission of the church becomes personalized in that sense, as it involves the whole of one's own self. The second level of mission begins with the Great Commission, that is, the commitment and desire to share person experience of grace with others. We cannot speak of church growth without understanding the mission (Mk 16: 15-16, Mt 28:19-20, Jn 20:21 and Jn 3:16). It refers to the on-going work of the Holy Spirit as a Pentecost experience (Acts 2: 1-12, 42-48). The mission includes the work of going into the world, making disciples, teaching and training them in the truth. To understand Church growth, we must look at the basic foundation of the church, which is, faith in Christ. A basic requirement for church growth is for us as Christians is to love Christ, be loyal and show commitment to Him and to His mission and vision of the church. For the church to grow, the servant leader has to take various positions, as systems of operation for action.

Sense of Purpose for the Common Good

The servant leader whether lay or clergy must be focused, to the point that, he or she will see the needs of the congregation from various visual points. The goal at all times, is not to be hurt or nor hurt any member of the congregation but to serve and build the common good. The sense of the purpose of the church is maintained by keeping the vision of God for the church in focus, applied to the context and needs of the people. This means that, the servant leader and with other servant leaders will transform all forms of conflicts, with the goal of promoting genuine love. This also means that, when changes have to be done or Revisioning of mission is done, all will be involved in the dialogue for change. Continuity, congruency and consistency of purpose and alignment among the members must remain spiritually meaningful, cohesive comprehensible and manageable. In terms of meaning, the mission must be remaining in the domain of personal passion and worthiness of investing all the necessary resources. In terms of comprehension, the mission and its activities must doable and within reality, even when self-sacrifice is seen as a necessity. In terms of management, mission and its organizational structure, requires that mission and its activities be organized with a clear sense of distribution of authority, to shape the beginning and the process of control to the destined end. In terms of cohesion, the mission and its purpose for growth must be seen and experienced as cohesive with focused activities, active involvement in the processes, and in the creation of a passionate imagination for all involved.

Reality, Mature Interactions and Use of Gifts and Abilities

Mission and its activities require taking a step of faith, and trusting God for the impossible. Yet, reality of the matters involved must be the interest of all servant leaders. The opportunities of ministry must be acted upon in concrete terms and specific actions to maintain clarity, integrity and cohesion.

Adhering to the common foundation will protect all Christians including church leaders from going astray. There are two common errors that Christians make: feeling too self-righteous with our gifts or feeling left out because we have no gift. First, we must guard against being too ego-centric (self-centered) and proud because of our abilities and gifts. Instead, we should appreciate that these gifts, talents, and abilities are intended for the common good. Second, we must not think of ourselves as observers with nothing to offer. Every Christian has something to offer to the ministries of the church.

What this means is that, every Christian has moods, attitudes, beliefs, feelings, and behaviors that affect the working relationships and fellowship. To remain healthy in the various activities and work of ministry, enough space must be provided within agreed boundaries for all members to be spontaneous, intensely involved and be whole-heartedly passionate about mission. The servant leaders and the members must work against depressive moods of hiding one from the other, acting out in ways that hurt each other, or live in rigidity, negative pessimism, and defocused imbalances.

The bible states that there are gifts of diversity and not of difference (1 Cor 12: 4ff). Diversity in gifts means that each person has been given a gift according to his or her needs (Gal 3:26-29). These gifts include wisdom, knowledge, faith, healing, miracles, prophesy, discernment of spirits, speaking in tongues, and interpretation of tongues. Individual identities and differences are complementary and enhance the growth that God intended for the church. In that sense, maturity of the church and its members will require them to engage in the natural processes of maturing, allowing healthy attachments and differentiation, going together through the stages and seasons of growing. The church is home in season and out of season. The church is home in "Good Friday Experiences" when there is pain and death. The church also lives in the quiet moments of "Holy Saturday" when all we need is the ministry of presence to each other. The church is also home on the "Easter Sunday" when there is confusion and new life is born in the church.

Reconciliation Message

The message of reconciliation is preached to restore all persons to unity in God, and one another. This ministry is only possible if we

trust in the name, and ministry of Jesus Christ Himself. The reconciliation mission is also expressed in the following terms:
1. Identity (in Christ)
2. Purpose (of reconciliation)
3. Ministerial functions – these include worship, preaching, evangelism fellowship, discipleship and teaching, and reaching out to the needy in community.
4. Promotion of sincere and honest life of justice, peace and love among all people
5. Pastoral functions – these include healing, reconciliation, guiding, sustaining, prophesying, tithe, discipleship, liberating and empowering.

Mission is also the work of God in action, where God meets people at their points of need (Lk 9: 1-2). Our identity and even vocation are an integral part of our mission because they are all given to us by God (Ex 3:10, Jn 20:21).

Titus Presler in his book, *Horizons of Mission* (2001) suggests a composite list of ten aspects of church growth.[1] These include: preaching the Gospel; serving sacrament; living as companions; being pilgrims; nurturing all dimensions of humanness; struggling for justice, peace, and reconciliation; being partners in collaboration; expressing the Gospel in diversity of culture; cooperating with persons of other faiths, and celebrating as a Eucharistic community. These new ways of engaging mission show that, a growing church will have to engage in natural healing, renewing and regenerating, as processes of healing itself naturally as all members walk with God in the garden or in the desert.

Recently, a friend of mine told me a story of people walking through the desert, and another group riding their camels through the desert. As evening approached, both groups came to a halt, and heard a voice: step down, and take sand and put it into your pockets.

---
[1] Titus Presler, *Horizons of Mission*: 155-177.

So they did, some reluctantly and others seriously. "The nights have a lot of wind and mornings are cold, this sand will make you glad and sad, tomorrow," said the voice. When morning came, the sand was gold. Some were sad and others were glad. This is a lesson for servant leaders and the members of the congregation, the time is now, use the strengths and resources that God has given you in your context.

Participatory and Observatory Positions of Servant Leadership
To stay focused on mission and growth, the servant leader (s) must be purposeful and meaningfully engaged, Sprit-directed, and meeting people at their points of need in ministerial and pastoral functions. The servant leader must also stay focused on message of reconciliation, be reality-oriented and have mature interactions with members and encourage genuine love among the members. To fulfill all these demands for mission, the servant leader (s) must regular shift the points of observation and participation to allow for a comprehensive approach. All these positions have a ministry of presence that hold the community in an interdependent relationship and partnership.

There are six positions that one can take to enhance belonging, participation and relationships with boundaries. The first position is being in front of the congregation. This position is altar-oriented where the leader is at the front of the congregation. The servant leader can be seen and can see the people. From this position, the servant leader pulls the people together and to himself or herself by mutual attraction to the grace of God and to the shared ministry. There is grace that comes with the regular worship that emanates and germinates for the altar.

The second position is from the back of the congregation. Most church have either the baptismal font or pool, or water from baptism. The servant leader shepherds and warmly welcomes, and says "farewell or dismissal" from the back. The servant leader sends forth the congregation into the world. This is a point of hospitality and warmth. By sending forth, the servant leader realizes that, the sheep and goats belong to the Lord of Lords and King of Kings, and that they are not his or her own. The servant leader is also a reactor who acts upon God's will for the congregation. This position will lead the servant leader to pray regularly for the members of the congregation during the week when various aspects of spiritual life are enhanced, encouraged and challenged.

The third position is when the servant leader is positioned within and among the members. The pastor here is experienced as a brother or sister in the faith. The pastor leads and serves as a believer, as a person, as a human being, as thinking and physical person, with feelings and emotions, and with needs like all other Christians. The active imagination of taking this position is a humbling experience, yet an experience of a servant leader who is relational with warmth and compassion, showing and living out love as shown in Christ Himself who became man and lived among us.

The fourth position is the pastor being positioned on the sides. This is the position of gathering as the mother hen gathers the chicks or as the open hands of Christ of the crucifix gather us to Himself. The pastor from this position will also protect the flock from all attacks that come from the sides of life. The pastor will guard with a garrison mentality, against idolatry, false teaching and false doctrine. From this position, the pastor takes the pulse, by thinking and feeling as a person who knows the threats to the sheep. Fifth position is the over-view position. This is metaphorically and physically being at the pulpit. The pastor from this position is high above, seeing functional systems of groups in the congregation. The pastor sees healthy and unhealthy dynamics in the congregation as various clusters of ministry are engaged in action. From this bird's view, the servant leader sees crisis, risks and challenges of immaturity that challenge the congregation and its ministries. From this point the pastor will see loyalty and commitment in action, in terms of opportunities and possibilities of ministry.

The sixth of the servant leader is the Gethsemane position. Here the pastor stands alone and way as Jesus did on many occasions when He needed a dialogue and conversation the God, the

Father. The pastor needs time of retreat, prayer, reflection and discernment for personal and communal action. Christ taught us that, Christians and their leaders need time for retreat, refreshment, renewal and re-energizing.

In analyzing these positions of leadership, I became more aware that, servant leaders are essential and integral agents for church growth, as they engage passionate in the mission of the church. They must continually analyze their positions and make the necessary paradigm shifts to care, nurture, feed, protect, relate and guard the flock of God given to their ministry. See Eph. 4:11, 1Peter 5:2, 1 Tim. 4:11-13, and 2Tim. 4:1-2. Pastors must continually shift their positions to communicate the word of God effectively, meeting the needs of individuals and the community. See Rom. 12:7, 1Corin. 12; 18 and Eph. 4:11.

In October 2009, Jesus Alive Ministries, Nairobi welcome a man into their congregation. The phenomenon brought a lot of young people. This group came from 5am in the morning and by 10am, they had filled the church before the regular attendees. As I watched this drama on television, I wondered, about different kinds of church growth. This rapid growth by circumstance was unprecedented. The fruits of this growth are yet to be seen. As a child of a peasant farmer, I saw growth of "coffee suckers." These were usually pruned and thrown away. This is unwanted growth which leads to destruction of productivity. There is also parasitic growth, growth that lives and thrives at the expense of others. The measuring of balanced growth is self-supporting, self-governing, self-propagating and self-serving, and reaching out to outsiders, who are needy, abused or neglected.

In 2007, a group of sixty five Presbyterians approached one of our church leaders, suggesting that, they wanted to join the Anglican Church. Upon further consultations, these persons were received into the Anglican Church. This is called malignant growth, that is, growth due to illnesses. What we have to see now is whether, this group will propagate further illnesses, or growth in healthy ways for Christian mission. I have suggested in this book that, Kenyan

Christian leaders are spiritual ethnic leaders, as "tribal chiefs." The church they grow follows the pattern of "homogenous growth." This is growth due to ethnic and cultural bonds. This "one-kind Mentality" or monocultural system of growth has to grow toward heterogeneity and cross-pollination.

As I make a transition to part two of this book, I hope the reader has experienced in this first section, the meaning, perspectives and systems of church growth. The second section deals with the biblical understanding of servant and leader in the church. The third section will focus on church leadership in Kenya.

Part Two: The New Testament Understanding of Leadership

CHAPTER EIGHT

Survey of the New Testament Concept of Leadership

Introduction

The tremendous growth of the church all over the world calls for better management of church affairs. This would follow the example of the industrialized countries which have put millions of dollars into management science. There are two viewpoints on the use of the development science as seen in the following statement:

> There is much to be gained by a continuing dialogue between the churches and secular organizations on the subject of leadership, . . . There remains, finally, one radical difference between the exercise of leadership in the church compared to any other organization. The importance of the model of the body lies in its focus on Christ Himself. The ultimate authority for the Christian is neither a code of Laws nor a Doctrinal system but Christ Himself . . . the fundamental task of Christian Leadership is through its practice, to allow the leadership of Christ to be made real effective, to be a channel for His leadership.[1]

There are these two views of either sticking to biblical leadership principles only, or using biblical leadership principles plus the skills of management science which do not conflict with the biblical norms of leadership.

---

[1] Peter Nott, "Towards a Theology of Leadership," *Expository Times*, 97 February 1996: 141-142.

Our view is the second one because we believe that the scriptural and Apostolic sources remain the criteria by which we judge the viability of the management science developments. The leadership needs of the church have grown from that of guiding a small band of disciples on the day of Pentecost to overseeing a big and complex church. Due to the ever changing complexity of modern Christian society, Christians have undergone human development in physical, social, spiritual, and economic area. Their lives in general move according to the life-style of recent times. Their thought patterns have changed with time. Their needs and habits have changed too. They have adopted new ways of life, and look at life with new views. This means, then, that for the church to meet the needs of her membership or to minister to the exact needs, leadership must be seriously enhanced. In addition, the African church has grown rapidly. Peter Falk pointed out in 1979 that the African church "membership is over 30 percent and could possibly reach 50 percent by the year 2000."[2] This growth of the church was seen by a statistician, researching on churches in Africa, who wrote in 1970 and said, "Africa may well have become in the main Christian continent . . . and the home of one of the larger Christian communities in the world."[3]

Jonathan Hildebrandt, writing on the position of the church in Africa in 1976 said, "our study has shown that Christianity started as a candle of light in Africa, but has now grown to a cloud of fire, giving light and direction to a great continent."[4] The same author, writing of the growth of the church in Kenya said, "In 1976, it was estimated that the population of Kenya was 13,797,000. The population today is estimated at 40Million. This also implies the number of

---

[2]Peter Falk, *The Growth of the Church in Africa*, Grand Rapids, Michigan: Zondervan Publishing House, 1979, 15.

[3]David B. Barret, "AD 200:350 Million Christians in Africa," *International Review of Missions,* 59 (1970): 39-54.

[4]Jonathan Hildebrandt, *History of the Church in Africa*, Achimota, Ghana: African Christian Press, 1981, 247.

Christians has grown. Sixty-six percent of the citizens of Kenya are considered Christian in practice or association"[5]

The church has to remain in the scriptures and draw out from them leadership principles to enhance her leadership, so that she can be more effective in her ministry. The leadership style of the church must come from angle of recognizing the inherent value of the individual, as well as recognizing the worth of human relations and the vision and design of God for servant leadership. Kenneth Gangel wrote,

> The church should be the most person-centered organization in the world ... The church which has its vertical relationships in order (Theo-centricity) will generally follow with proper horizontal relationships (anthro-centricity) ... sometimes we get so busy 'saving souls' that we forget to do anything for the people.[6]

The church leadership must first be Theo-centric (centered of God and according to the will of God as seen in the Holy Scriptures), and then anthro-centric (centered on man, meeting the social and spiritual needs of man) aspects will follow. Church leadership must be exercised according to the will of God and according to the pattern He has set forth (Theo-centricity). Leadership has to be anthro-centric, centered around the welfare of the person that is being led, but not upon the person who is leading. New Testament leadership is a God centered leadership and a Christian-centered leadership

Overview of the New Testament Concept of Leadership

To be able to improve our understanding of Leadership in the New Testament, we shall briefly survey church leadership in the Gospels, the book of Acts, and in the General Epistles. In this survey we shall try to establish the form, function, principles, and patterns of

---

[5] Ibid., 256
[6] Kenneth O. Gangel, *Competent to Lead*, Chicago: Moody Press, 1974), 10.

church leadership. We shall also bear in mind that the church is both an organism and an organization, a duality that may impact church leadership. The basic idea of "Leadership" that we shall survey may be defined as, "the means by which authority is made effective. [7] We shall attempt to deal with the personal qualities of a leader and the functions of leadership, both of which make a leader an effective servant of God and of the church. Leadership may be defined broadly as "any behavior which helps the group to meet stated goals or fulfils its purpose"[8], and a leader as "anyone who is assigned to provide such behavior or who emerges in an extra ordinary way to do so on his or her own".[9]

Survey of Leadership in the New Testament Historical Books

Jesus is the model of a Leader as Seen in the Gospels. In thinking of New Testament leadership style, the model of our Lord Jesus Christ is the enormous and overruling example which is to be emulated by every Christian leader. Every Christians, as well as every Christian leader, must be imitator of Jesus Christ (Eph. 5:1).

To Christ, leadership is service. Service humbles the leader rather than exalts him (John 13:3-17 and Phil. 2:1-11). His kind of service sets an example. He was willing to wash His disciples' feet. He taught His followers how to serve, and He demanded no less of those who would carry on His work on earth. Ted Engstrom, writing on the making of a Christian leader, states: "He makes it clear that true leadership is grounded in love which must issue in service."[10]

---

[7]Nott, 138.

[8]A. Duane Litfin, "The Nature of the Pastoral Role." B*ibliotheca Sacra 139* (January – March 1982): 60.

[9]Ibid.

[10]Ted W. Engstrom, *The Making of a Christian Leader*, (Grand Rapids, Michigan: Zondervan Publishing House, 1976), 37.

Both Gangel and Engstrom, who are well known Christian writers on church leadership, agree that New Testament leadership according to Luke 22:24 – 27 and Mark 10:45 is not political power-play' in the church (pre-eminence among), nor is it 'exercising lordship' (authoritarian control over the minds and behavior of other people). New Testament leadership is not cultic control, public relations, or platform personality, but humble service to Christians. Leadership of Christ is, ". . . focused on individuals (John 21) . . . focused on scriptures (Matt. 5:21-48), focused on Himself on Himself (John 14:9) . . . and focused on purpose."[11]

To Jesus, a leader does the work of serving and is therefore a servant. From this we can see that a leader is Servant-Leader (Luke 22:26). Matthew 20:25-28 shows that servant-hood is an essential tenet for one called to the ambitious position of a leader. Mark 10:35-45 and 22:24-27 emphasize the greatness and satisfaction the comes with being a servant (see also Mark 9:35)

Matthew 23:1-10 negates the idea of the leader which was eminent among the Pharisees and the Scribes. They told others what to do but they did not do it themselves (v. 3). They made rules and regulations for others but they were not bound, or were unwilling, to follow them (v. 4).They did whatever they did to be noticed by men (v. 5). They wanted leadership positions with the aim of getting themselves the seats of honor in banquets and in synagogues (v. 6). They wanted to gain respect in respectful greetings (v. 7, see Matt 26:25, 49; Mark 9:5, 10:51, 11:21, and John 1:38, 49; 3:2, 4:31; 6:25; 9:2; 11:8; 20:16). They wanted to gain the title of *rabbi* (v. 7). But Jesus expected otherwise from His disciples. They were to be different in their concept of leadership. They were to be different and, in fact, the complete opposite of the Pharisees and scribes. They were all brothers (v. 8) with one Father in heaven, with one Leader and Teacher (Jesus Christ, vv. 8-10). For them, the greatest was one who was a servant and who was humble, not one who was served and proud.

---

[11] Ibid., 172-173.

In summary, we see that, to Jesus Christ, leadership meant servant-hood. This clearly shows us that His view of leadership is different from all ordinary standards used in the twentieth century. In spite of this earnest warning in the Gospels, many church leaders through church history have loved leadership, plus pre-eminence, at the expense of responsibility, accountability, and loyalty to God.

Leadership in the Early Church Seen in the Book of Acts

The book of the Acts is very vivid in describing the life of the early church. But it must be noted that the church then was still in its early stages. Before the missionary expansion of the church, recorded in the second part of the book of Acts (chapters 13-28), church leadership was yet highly not developed. The model of a servant – leader was fully developed, but the methods were not yet completed. The disciples had learnt about servant-hood from the Master-Servant, Jesus Christ, and they had in turn to pass this on. The structure of the early New Testament church unfolded itself through the leadership of committed men who were steered and spear-headed by the apostles. Despite the fact that the leadership system was structurally under-developed, the Christians of that era turned the world up-side down for Christ. We learn much about early church leadership in Acts because of the practicability of the methods used. The early church leaders had a unique strategy, or a unique motivation, for leadership' because they effectively reached many of their generation. Acts is primarily a historical narrative rather than a developed ecclesiological account, but this does not call for a minimizing of its contribution to the understanding of vital leadership tenets for the church of Christ.

In the early chapters of Acts, the apostle Peter was the leader of the church in Jerusalem. Peter's sermon, on the day of Pentecost, gives us two important tenets which are the pre-requisites of every Christian leader: a personal commitment to the lordship of Christ and the empowering of the Holy Spirit. The following chapters continue to portray Peter as one of the accepted leaders of the apostolic band (Acts 1:15).

Acts 6 is a passage which concerns leadership as it records the choosing of the seven deacons. The church was growing and the Greek-speaking widows (who spoke the common Greek dialect and acquainted with Greek habits of life and education) were being overlooked in the daily distribution of food. The apostles asked the church to choose from herself seven men. The qualifications needed for such men were that they were full of the Holy Spirit and full of wisdom. I. H. Marshall, commenting on this passage, wrote:

The seven men were therefore appointed to take charge of the work, and were installed by the laying on of hands. It is noteworthy that spiritual qualifications were sought in men appointed to such tasks within the church . . . the solution to the problem was the appointment of a new group of leaders to serve tables . . . the men chosen were to be distinguished by their possession of wisdom (6:3,10) and the Spirit, that is, a wisdom inspired by the Spirit . . . the proposal made by the twelve was put before a church and gained their approval.[12]

There is a clear indication that the choice of the seven candidates was made by the members of the church and not by the apostles themselves. The apostles appointed them by praying for them and placing or laying of hands upon them. This rite indicated a conferring of authority on them.

As the church continued to grow, an organized leadership became necessary. In Acts 15, the council of Jerusalem had to be organized to deal with the divisive and sharp issue of circumcision. James, the brother of our Lord, is seen as the leader of the church in Jerusalem, but we noticed that he consulted with the other apostles and elders.

In Acts, the offices of ministry mentioned are the apostle, prophet, evangelist, shepherd, and teacher (Acts 15:2,4,6 and 21:8). We shall devote a whole section on the study of these offices in a later part of our thesis. A leadership tenet that we learn from this

---

[12]I. Howard Marshall, *The Acts of the Apostles,* (Grand Rapids, Michigan: William B. Eerdmans Publishing Company, 1980), 125-126.

chapter is the authority and discipline was exercised over assemblies and individuals, but not in a totalitarian manner. It was done lovingly. People accepted those in authority, not because they had to or were under compulsion, but because they wanted to (Acts 15:1-35). We learn that leadership was an all-people' movement which resulted in team worK (Acts 13:1, 1-4; 14:23; 15:32, 40 and 16:1-3).

Leadership involves the use of other people in the decision making process. In Acts 20:17 and 28 the apostle Paul called the elders of the Ephesians church to encourage, consult, and discuss issues on church leadership. Here is an excellent example of organized leadership. The three aspects of one ministry are portrayed: the elders were task was that of overseeing the church, and they had to do the ministry of shepherding.

Survey of Leadership in the General Epistles

Since this is a brief survey, for the purpose of this thesis, only Hebrews 13:7, 17 James 5:14 and 1 pet. 5:1-4 will be considered.

Hebrews 13:7 exhorts the Hebrews to keep in remembrance of their former leaders, to abide steadfastly their teaching. In Heb. 2:3 and 4:2 these leaders spoke the word of the gospel to the Hebrews. These leaders must have been influential men in who some undefined authority was vested. We are only told that they were leaders. Official status *per se* was not yet defined and official titles *per se* were not yet universal. The chief reason for their being held in remembrance and honor was "their manner of life," that is, their conduct. These leaders had sealed their teaching and exhibited a faith worthy of imitation. Here lies yet another challenge for church leaders: they must live a manner of life worthy of their leadership. They must be careful because leadership influences the people that are being led.

Hebrews 13:17, which is within the concluding and exhorting part of the epistle, injects the need for a positive and responsible attitude towards leaders. This second mention of leaders suggests that there were leaders of the church, but no hint is given as to what offices they held.

The writer of the epistle is concerned only about attitudes, and mentions two which are complementary to each other: obedience *(peithesthe)* and submission *(hypeikete)*. These Christians were admonished to obey their present leaders and yield themselves trustfully to their teaching. A writer said, "The function of leaders is mentioned in general terms as "keeping watch over those committed to their care."[13]

This meant that whatever these leaders were doing was in the interest of the souls of the people they were leading. It also implies that the leaders were sacrificing some of their personal interests for the sake of the people they were leading. Those being led, by implication, equally needed to sacrifice some of their interests for the sake of their leaders. We learn that church leaders have a heavy responsibility of watching over the souls of the people they are leading. This 'watching' means feeding and shepherding them. This challenges leaders in our churches to do this work of 'watching,' and not that of destroying or milking.

We see, in this passage, that the office of a leader is recognized as one of responsibility, for those who hold such office will be expected to give account of their work. Here is a big motivation for all Christian leaders as they minister to the souls of Christians. This does show us that there is or there should be an inner voice, or consciousness of pressure, because one day leaders must render an account to the chief shepherd (Heb. 13:20). Those who exercise authority must also accept responsibility for their actions. Leaders are to perform their task or duties joyfully. This will only happen if they do so 'not with groaning' *(mestenazontes)*. Leaders will not effectively do work which is thankless, unappreciated, and even opposed, although this is what Christ Himself experience (John 1:11). The idea of leadership with groaning is not welcome, nor is to be

---

[13]Donald Guthrie, *The Letter to the Hebrews,* (Grand Rapids, Michigan: William B. Eerdmans Publishing Company, 1983), 276-277.

encouraged, because it would be of no advantage, and it would not profit either those leading or those being led.

James 5:14 deals with the prayer of faith. It would be unfair to read too much into the context to make it have something to do with leadership, but it has something worth noting. Here we have something unique; in James, namely, a concrete reference to the official organization of the Christian community, the church, under the rule of elders. The combination of the two terms, *Presbyteroi* and *ekklesias*, points to a developed organization among communities of the *diaspora*, and this same idea was borrowed for use in the epistle. It is pre-supposed that, by virtue of their office, the elders had prayers with a particular efficacy. These elders are leaders of the church. Their going and praying for the sick person represents the entire church.

The leader, according to James, has a heavy responsibility of praying for the sick. This adds to our list of duties for a church leader. Though the elders (leaders) are to pray for the sick, this verse cannot be appealed to as evidence that the Lord has committed to His church for all time the power of miraculous healing. One author commented,

> We cannot deduce from this verse that anointing of the sick with oil, consecrated by priests, should for Christians supplement, as a matter of course, the work of medical practitioners in the healing of disease, or be regarded as a means of sacramental benediction when hope for cure through ordinary channels has been abandoned. Unction is therefore not to be regarded as a sacrament, for it was not ordained by Christ Himself to be a permanent institution of His church.[14]

From the day of the Pentecost, Peter, the apostle of Jesus Christ, was one of the accepted leaders of the church. He had great influence upon the early church, so to ponder his advice, which he wrote

---

[14]R. V. G. Tasker, *The General Epistle of James* (Grand Rapids, Michigan: William B. Eerdmans Publishing Company, 1983), 131.

in his years of Christian maturity, is a valuable exercise. He wrote these guides to a persecuted church, and these form part of the timeless principles which every types of Christian leader must feel obliged to apply in the leadership.

I Peter 5:1-4 shows us Peter's exhortation to the elders, who are in fact under-shepherds, committed to the primary responsibility of feeding and caring for the flock of God, which God committed to their care. Peter did not write to these elders as 'chief of the apostle', but as 'fellow elder' who was bearing similar responsibilities. He spoke to them not from above, but from along-side. Here we learn a good ground for exercising leadership. A shepherd's work cannot be done effectively without a shepherd's heart. Peter, in this passage, is dealing with the motivation of these official heads of the communities, to which this epistle is addressed. The spiritual leaders is to assume and discharge his responsibility unforced, not under compulsion, but willingly, and not because he feels he cannot get out of it.

In 1 Pet, 5:2, Peter charges these elders with the very charge he received from the Lord (John 21:19). This is what all church leaders, without exception, are charged with. In this same verse, Peter tells them to 'shepherd the flock of God.' Many times church leaders need to be reminded that the Christians they serve are God's flock, not their own.

The ministry of shepherding is heavy responsibility for the under-shepherd, who is called and sent by the chief shepherd, who is Christ Himself. He must follow the chief shepherd, in terms of vision, mission and practice of leadership.. The human part of the under-shepherd must not be put into use in the ministry. His preferences and desires must not be imposed on the sheep that are being led.

Peter emphasizes three important factors to be considered by a Christian leader. Such a leader should work voluntarily and willingly, not like one under compulsion; he should do the ministry according to the will of God; and he should do the ministry with eagerness, devotion, and zeal. To Peter, ministry must be done:

(i) for the right reason, or in the right spirit, not because they must, but because they freely choose to do so; (ii) with the right motive, not for material gain, but for the sheer delight of doing it, that is, finding satisfaction in the job itself rather that in what in what they get out of it; (iii) in the right manner, not driving but leading, not domineering but setting an example; (iv) with a proper awareness that in it, they serve the Chief Shepherd to whom they are answerable and He will Himself reward service with rewards that are eternal.[15]

With these facts in mind, we can begin to shape our view of Christian leadership. These tenets for leadership are eternal standards which do not change. Therefore, they applied then, and they still apply today, for all Christian leaders. Christian leadership is humble ministry of service, but not love of power or love of authority.

---

[15]A. M. Stibbs and A. F. Walls, *The First Epistle General of Peter* (Grand Rapids, Michigan: William B. Eerdmans Publishing Company, 1983), 165.

CHAPTER NINE

New Testament Vocabulary for Servant-Leadership

Introduction

New Testament focuses on leadership service (*diakonia*). Second, the New Testament focuses on leadership as an aspect of worship and devotion (*latria*). These two main thoughts inform the ministry of leaders and servants of God and of humanity and other creation.

The *Diaconal* Word Group

Diakoneo

The term *diakoneo* has been used in the New Testament with a range of meanings: wait on someone at table (Luke 12:37, 17:8), serve someone, that is, giving any kind of service (Matt. 4:11, 27:55, Mark 10:45); care for or take care of (Acts 6:2, 2 cor.3:3); help or support someone (Matt. 25:44 Luke 8:3, Rom. 15:25, Heb. 6:10); and of the ecclesiastical office as a deacon (1 Tim.3:10).[1]

---

[1] William F. Arndt and F. Wilbur Gingrich, *A Greek-English Lexicon of the New Testament and other Early Christian Literature* (Chicago, Illinois: The University of Chicago Press, 1957), 183.

Matthew 8:15, Mark 1:31, Luke 4:39, 10:40, John 12:2, Luke 17:8, and Acts 6:2 use *diaconeo* to mean 'serving at table'. Matt. 27:55, Mark 15:41, Luke 8:3, Matt. 4:11, and use *diaconeo* in the sense of taking care of individuals. 2Tim. 1:18, Heb. 6:10, and 1 pet. 4:10 use the term in the context of serving within the church.[2]

The term *diaconeo* is used to mean service, that is, doing the work of a deacon (1 Tim. 3:10, as an ecclesiastical office).[3] This service comes from love for those being served. The original meaning is seen in Luke 17:8 and John 12:2, where it is used to mean 'to wait at table,' but in Luke 22:26 Jesus Christ astonished His disciples because He reversed the normally known ethical behavior. He was the master, the Teacher who was to be served, yet He Himself served. This particular incident has affected the usage of this term, especially when used in the context of the church. We take the view that the deacon did the work of serving. He provided for the needs of the people he served. The emphasis of this term, when applied to a Christian leader, is that he provides for the needs of the people he is leading.

The meaning of *diaconeo* is best demonstrated by the person and ministry of Christ Himself, as well as by the nature of the gospel itself. To us, this term denotes a loving action for a brother or for a neighbor which in turn is derived from the divine love of God. It also describes the outworking of Koinonia, fellowship.

Looking at 1 Tim. 3:10, we note that the work of a deacon developed, into a special office of leadership. The ministry of a deacon had the responsibility of material care in the church, to a more complex office of bishop, who expressed his role in public worship, care for the poor, and administration.

---

[2] *The New International Dictionary of New Testament Theology* 1978 en., s.v. "Serve," by K. Hess.

[3] F.Wilbur Gingrich, *Shorter Lexicon of the Greek New Testament* (Chicago: The University of Chicago press, 1983), 46.

Diakonia

The shorter Lexicon defines *diakonia* as service in general (Acts 6:4, 2 Cor. 4:12, Eph. 4:12, Heb 1:14, and Rev. 2:19), of domestic service (Luke 10:40), of service in office or ministry (Acts 1:17, 20:24, Rom. 12: 5, 1 Cor. 5:18), of aid, support, distribution (Acts 6:1, 11:29), and contribution (2 Cor. 9: 2) 12. Others define *diakonia* as service in general (Luke 10:40), service in the office of a prophet or an apostle 1 Tim. 1:12, Acts 1:17 aid or support or distribution, especially of alms and charitable giving (Acts 6:1) and of the office of a deacon (Rom. 12:7)[4]

The term *diaconia* is used thirty-four times in the New Testament. It is mainly used to mean serving at table. Generally *diaconia* is used of loving service. The loving service can be shown by making a collection (Acts 11:29, 12:25), by proclamation of the word and the Christian commission (2 Tim. 4:11, Acts 6:4), and by all services in Christian communities (Eph. 4:12)[5]

We are of the view that the term *diakonia* emphasizes service. This term, when used of a Christian leader, connotes that he is there to serve. The business of a church leader is serving, aiding, and supporting in the area that God has called him to.

Diakonos

Diakonos is found twenty-nine times in the New Testament. Its primary connotation is a servant. It is used of domestic servants (John 2:5,9) of the civil ruler (Rom. 13:4), of Christ (Rom. 15:8, Gal. 2:17), of the followers of Christ in relation to one another (Matt. 20:26, 23:11, Mark 9:35 10:43), of the servants of Christ in the work of preaching and teaching (1 cor. 3:5, 2 cor. 3:, 6:4, 11:23, Eph.3:7), and of those who serve in churches (Rom.16:1)[6] The term is used of a servant (Matt. 20:26), a helper (1 Thess. 3:2), an official of the

---

[4] Arndt and Gingrich, *Lexicon*, 183.
[5] Hess, "Serve,"
[6] Arndt and Gingrich, *Lexicon*, 183-184.

church (1 Tim. 3:8, 13, Titus 1:9), a helper (agent) of government authorities (Rom. 13:4), and a deaconess.[7]

Generally, a *diakonos* is a person who serves at table. He is a servant in the wider sense, as in Matt. 20:26 and Mark 10:43, or a helper as in Eph. 6:21.

The Pauline usage of *diakonos* includes: a servant of the new covenant a (2 Cor. 3:6); a servant of righteousness (2 Cor. 11:15); a servant of the gospel (Eph. 3:7); a servant of the church (col.1:25); and of a man holding the office of deacon in the church (Phil. 1:1, 1 Tim. 3:8-13).[8]

The *Latria* word Group

Latreuo

The shorter Lexicon defines *latreia* as religious service or worship of God (John 16:2, Rom. 9:4, 12:1, and Heb. 9:1), and *latreuo* as to serve by carrying out religious duties (Matt. 4:10, Luke 1:74, Acts 7:7, Rom. 1:9, and 2 Tim. 1:3)[9] *Latreuo* is defined as, "To serve, carrying out religious duties (of cultic nature) by human beings."[10] Rom. 1:25 and Acts 7:42 indicate the manner in which such service is performed.

The term *latreuo* primarily refers to work for hire, and signifies worship or to serve. Of worship, it is used of service to God (Matt.4:10), to God and Christ (Rev.22:3), in the tabernacle (Heb. 8:5), or to the host of heaven (Acts 7:47).[11] Though the term *latreuo* is used 21 times in the New Testament, in the religious sense it has been carried from Old Testament, and has the connotation of serv-

---

[7]*An Expository Dictionary of New Testament Words*, s. v. "Deacon." By W. E. Vine.

[8] Hess, "Serve,"

[9]Gingrich, *Shorter Lexicon*, 117.

[10]Arndt and Gingrich, *Lexicon*, 468.

[11]Hess, "Serve,"

ing or worshipping God, not for wages, but out of gratitude for God's acts of salvation in history.[12]

Paul, in Rom. 1:9, had given himself to the life of service to God. His motivation was not wages, but the fact that he was serving God. The motivation for a Christian leader, though serving men, is that he is serving God. In the New Testament this term is used of prophets and teachers in Antioch who ministered to the Lord (Acts. 13:2); the duty of churches to minister to the Jewish saints at Jerusalem (Rom. 15:27); and to official service of priests and Levites under the Law (Heb. 10:11). This term primarily has to do with fulfillment of an office or the discharge of a function.[13]

Leitourgeo
The term *leitourgeo* is the compound of *loa* (meaning, "people") and *ergon* (meaning "work"). It is normally used for a political or legal concept. When used in this sense, it means to do public work at one's own expense. When used in religious sense, it expresses a service of people to God seen in their relationship to Him.[14]

In Rom. 15:16, Paul expresses his complete dedication and dependence upon God; by God's grace he had become Christ's priest to the Gentiles. Paul redefines the nature of sacrifice and priestly service in terms of the gospel. In Phil. 2:25 and 30, *Epaphroditus* had become a *leitourgos*, that is, a helper. He served Paul in his hour of need. He rendered Paul a service, which the church, owing to circumstances, was not able to render.

The term refers to the performance of public service. This service could be in public office, or in religious or ritual service. It can refer to service performed by priests and Levites in the temple (Heb. 10:11), or to Christian services (Titus 1:9). Figuratively, it can refer to the various ways in which the religious man serves God (Acts 13:2). It can be used generally to refer to the service (Rom.

---

[12]*Expository Dictionary*, s.v. "Serving,".
[13]Hess, "Serve,"
[14]*Expository Dictionary*, s. v. , "Minister,".

15:27) of the officials of Christian church (prophets, teachers, bishops and deacons).[15]

Finally, *leitourgeo* can refer to working for Christ in the proclamation of the gospel, as well as the work of service to God and to the Christian community (Rom. 15:27) and 2 Cor. 9:12). We conclude with the view that when this term is used of Christian leaders, it emphasizes that in serving the people of God, we are serving God. This type of service must be done with complete dedication and complete dependence upon God. The service should include proclamation of the gospel, as well as works of service to the Christian ministry.

The Official Words of Leadership

Doulos

This term is defined as 'enslaved, enthralled, and subservient: as used in Rom. 6:19. In a bad sense, it refers to one involved in moral or spiritual thralldom, as used in John 8:34, Rom.6:17, 20, 1 Cor. 7: 23, and 2 Pet. 2:19. In a good sense it is used of a devoted servant, or minister, as in Acts 16:17, and Rom.1:1, or one pledged, or bound, to serve, as in 1 Cor. 7:22 and 2 Cor. 4:5.[16] Some authors define *doulos* as bondman or servant. The shorter Lexicon define *doulos* as slavish, servile, or slave.[17]

The general translation of *doulos* is servant, and this signified one that was in bondage, but the main idea was that of subjection. It is used of natural conditions (Matt. 8:9), 1 Cor. 7:21), and of spiritual, moral, and ethical conditions. It is used of servants of God, servants of Christ, servants of sin, and servants of corruption.[18]

In society, slaves were occasionally put in a position of responsibility and command (Matt. 24:45). The slave owed his master exclusive and absolute obedience (Matt. 8:9). His work earned him

---

[15]Hess, "Serve,'

[16]Arndt and Gingrich, *Lexicon*, 471-472.

[17]Gingrich, *Shorter Lexicon,* 51-52

[18]Arndt and Gingrich, *Lexicon*, 204.

neither profit nor thanks, and he did what he owed as a bond slave (Luke 17:7-10). The master could use his unlimited power over his slave for good or for bad (Matt. 18:27, and 25:30).[19]

We also bear in mind that the New Testament resists the contemporary verdict on slaves as a contemptible lower class by the way it uses *doulos* in the parables to describe the relation of all men to God. The New Testament portrays a harmonious relationship, which was to exist between the lord and the servant, but each had to maintain his place.

The *doulos* was different from the master (Matt. 8:9), from a freeman (1 Cor. 7:21), from the son (John 8:9), from a Christian brother (Philemon 16).

In the context of Matt. 20:27 and 23:11, the Christian leader is a *doulos* in relation to the people he is leading. The apostles were *doulos* of Christians, they were unconditionally obligated to serve them (2 Cor. 4:5). The slave did the most menial work. The position of a double was the lowest in the social ladder. The needs of others were always first. Personal freedom, personal expression, and personal identity were all denied (Matt.8:9). The emphasis of this title is servant-hood. A leader in the church of Christ is a servant.

Poimen

The term *poimen* is defined as 'one who tends flocks or herds, a shepherd, a herdsman' (Matt. 9:36, 25:32). It is metaphorically defined as 'a pastor superintendent, guardian' (John 10:11, 14, 16). *Poimen* literally means shepherd or sheepherder, as used in Matt.9:36, Mark 6:34, and Luke 2:8-15. It is used of Christ Himself, as well as for human leaders and for pastors (Eph. 4:11).[20] The term *poimen* can be used symbolically, as in Matt. 26:31, John 10:2, 11, 14, 16, and figuratively, as in Heb. 13: 20, 1 Pet. 2:25 and Eph. 4:11, meaning pastor.

---

[19]*Expository Dictionary*, s. v., "Servant,"
[20]*Dictionary of New Testament Theology*, s. v. "Slave," by R. Tuente.

In John 10:1-21, Luke 15:4-7, and Matt. 18:12-14, the shepherd's devotion to duty is painted in glorious colors. Here, also, we see Jesus is the Messianic shepherd, the Good Shepherd (see pet. 5:4 and Heb. 12:20). Jesus gathered the lost sheep of Israel (Matt. 9:36, 10:24, and Luke 19:10) Jesus died for the flock; He voluntarily laid down His life for them (Matt. 26:31 and Mark 14:27).[21]

We are of the view that a Christian leader is a *poimen*, because he does the work of 'caring for' the Christians. We are also of the view that, at the time of Christ, some shepherds did not do their shepherding well, and were the cause of some negative attitudes towards the shepherds (John 10:1-21). A according to John 10:3, Luke 15:4, and Matt. 18:12, a shepherd who was wholeheartedly devoted to his duty was respected. The Christian leader has to have a total devotion to the well being of the sheep, gather the sheep safely, treat them well, and know them well.

The Christian leader as *poimen* must follow the pattern of the master, the Great shepherd (1 pet. 5:4). He should give mild, gentle, caring, and driving guidance, and protect and allow liberty and freedom of activity. He must forget his heavy duty of feeding the sheep. The church leader's role is shepherding or pasturing, "the former term is derived from Anglo-Saxon and the latter from Latin, but both here come back to the relationship between a flock of sheep and the one who keeps them."[22]

From this study of *poimen*, we have one, and only one, Great shepherd. Nowhere do we learn of an organization, or one denomination, in which we all should be. There are many under-shepherds, but all are under the one Great Shepherd. For the church, "This shepherding image is regularly used in the New Testament to speak of the relationship between a congregation and its leaders (Acts 20: 28-29 1; Cor. 9:7, 4:11, 1 Pet. 5:1-4).[23]

---

[21]Gingrich, *Shorter Lexicon*, 75

[22]*Dictionary of New Testament Theology*, s. v. "Shepherd," by E. Beyreudther.

[23]Gingrich, *Shorter Lexicon*, 75.

Episkopos

The shorter Lexicon defines *episkopos* as overseer, guardian, or supervisor. This title is used of Jesus, in 1 Pet. 2:25. This title is also used for the term bishop, in a less technical manner, in referring to him as an official of the church (Acts 20:28, Phil. 1:1, Tim. 3:2, and Titus 1:7).[24]

The term *episkopos* is defined as an overseer, guarding, or bishop, while *episkopeo* describes the function of *epikcopos*, which is to take care, oversee, or care for. This term refers to visitation, affliction, position, or office as an overseer or bishop.[25] The term *episkopos* is compound from *epic*, meaning "over", and *skopeo* meaning, "to look or watch".[26] It was used of God as the creator and guardian of every soul (Job 20:29). It was also used of Christ as the guardian of souls (1 pet. 2:25). It is also used of persons who have a definite function or fixed office, as a superintendent, guardian, or bishop (Acts 20:28, Phil.1, 1 Tim. 3:2, Titus 1:7).[27]

The emphasis of this term seems to take on the activity of looking at, or paying attention to, a person or thing. The aspect of supervision is a duty of fellowship. In Acts 20:28, Phil 11, 1 Tim. 3:1 and Titus 1:7, this is used of Christian leaders in a Christian community.

In the Luke writings and in Heb. 2:6, the term *episkeptomai* is used for God's loving and seeking care. In Acts 7:23, and 15:3b, the term *episkeptomai* is used to stress Christian loving and seeing care with a heart is moved to action.

We are of the view that the overseeing work of a bishop involves loving care and concern. There is no doubt that this is a heavy responsibility, which must be shouldered by anyone who is called to the office of bishop. This office calls for selfless service,

---

[24] *Dictionary of New Testament Theology*, s. v. "Bishop," by L. Coenen.
[25] *Expository Dictionary*, s. v. "Bishop,"
[26] Arndt and Gingrich, *Lexicon*, 299.
[27] *Coenen*, "Bishop,".

and is never a way of personal aggrandizement. We believe this out of the conviction of 1 Tim. 3:1, where verse 1 speaks of the office, and verses 2-16 move the attention to the personal qualities of a bishop.

Presbyteros

The two forms of this term are *presbyteros* which means "be older, ambassador, or rule;" and *presbyteros* which "means council of elders, rank of elders, or elder."[28] *Presbyteries* is defined as elder, senior, older, more advanced in years or in respect of age (Luke 15:25, John 8:9, Acts 2:17 and 1 Tim. 5:1, 2). It also means an elder or a local dignitary (Luke 7:3), an elder or presbyter of the Christian church (Acts 11:30, 14:23). *Presbyteros* can mean elder, eldest, or old men, as well as a person of advanced age, and can be used a designation of an official, either among the Jews, or among Christian.[29] It refers to age or rank (position) of responsibility. When used to refer to leaders of Christian churches, the *presbyteros* was charged to exercise spiritual care and oversight.[30]

In Acts 11:30, 14:23, 15:2, 4, 6, 22, and 16:4 we see that there were elders in the church in Jerusalem. Their duties included, among other things, exhortation and preaching (Titus 1:5, James 5:14, 1 Pet. 5:1).[31] These men were older in age (see Luke 15:25), and were designated as officials of the church (1 Tim. 5:17).[32]

We are persuaded to believe that the terms *episkopos* and *presbyteros* carried the same meaning and were used interchangeably. The use of the title *presbyteros* is very appropriate with our understanding that an elder commands respect and authority on the ground of experience and wisdom.

---

[28]Gingrich, *Shorter Lexicon*, 167.
[29]*Expository Dictionary,* s. v. "Elder,"
[30]Arndt and Gingrich, *Lexicon*, 706
[31]Ibid., 707.
[32]Gingrich, *Shorter Lexicon*, 24.

We are of the view that as the church developed, the term *presbyteros* developed different senses. For example, in the synoptic gospels and at the beginning and end of the book of Acts, the subject is used of the lay members of the Sanhedrin. Another example is the central portion of Acts, the pastoral epistles, James 5:14, and the salutations in 2 and 3 John, where *presbyteries* is used for the Christian leader.

In conclusion, the term *presbyteros* was a title used to describe men who exercised leadership in the Christian church (Acts 11:26, 30). These men cared for the welfare of the members of the body, as well as for the life of the church. Though we notice that these had a judicial role, they had a special task of exhorting and refuting objectors (Acts 20:17, 28, James 5:14). The *presbyteros* was a bearer and deliverer of the apostolic tradition (2 John 1:1, 3 John 1:1), but his authority would solely lie in what he said in truth and in the power of the spirit.

Apostolos
The defining of this term is sometimes categorized in two ways. The first is that of delegate, envoy, or messenger, as in Luke 11:49, John 13:16, 2 Cor. 8:23, 8:23, Eph. 3:5, Phil. 2:25, Heb.3:1, Rev. 2:2, and 18:20. The second is of one holding the most responsible position of service in the Christian communities (1 Cor. 12:28), used especially of Jesus' original twelve disciples (Matt. 10:2, Acts 1:26 and Rev. 21:14). It is also used of prominent leaders outside the twelve, as in Acts 14:14, Rom. 1:1, 16:7, and Gal. 1:19.[33]

The term *apostolos* literally means one sent forth. It is compounded from two words: *apo*, meaning from, and *stello*, meaning to send. It is used Christ Himself in relation to God the Father (Heb. 3:1 and John 17:3). It is also used the twelve disciples chosen by the Lord (Luke 6:10). It is used by Paul (Acts 1:22), who was commis-

---

[33]*Expository Dictionary*, s. v. "Apostle, Apostleship,"

sioned by the Lord, after His ascension, to carry the gospel to the gentiles.[34]

In the New Testament we see this term used to mean delegate, envoy, messenger (John 13:16, Phil. 2:25, 2 Cor. 8:24), and missionary. It is especially used of God's messengers (Luke 11:49, Rev. 18:20, Eph. 3:5) and of a group of highly honored believers, who had a special function (apostles), such as Paul (Rom. 1:1), Barnabas (Acts 14:14), Andronicus and Jonas (Rom.16:7), James (Gal. 1:19), Peter (1 per. 1:1), the twelve apostles (Matt. 10:2, Mark 3:14), possessors of the most important spiritual gift (1 Cor. 12:28), and preachers of the gospel (2 Cor. 12:12).[35] As listed here, the general usage is messenger, but we see these men as fixed designation of a definite office. In Acts 6:6 and 15:2 the apostles guarded the true tradition about the Lord Jesus Christ.

The call and commissioning to the lifelong service of an apostle was through Jesus Christ and God the Father (Gal. 1:1). This only came through meeting to be delivered to men (1 Cor. 11:23, 2 Cor. 4:6, Gal. 1:12, and 2 Cor. 5:20). D. Muller notes, "Paul gives no suggestion that the apostles' special position exalts him above the church and distinguishes him from the other spiritual gifts (1 Cor. 4:16, Phil. 3:17, 1 Cor. 12:25-28)."[36]

We are of the view that the apostles were primarily pioneer preachers of the gospel, and they occupied unique positions of leadership and authority. They planted and superintended the work of the churches, commissioned local officers, administered discipline, and settled issues of general dispute (Acts 1:22, 14:4,7, 23, 15:1, 1 Cor. 9:1, and 1 Thesis. 2:6).

---

[34]Arndt and Gingrich, *Lexicon*, 99.

[35]*Dictionary of New Testament Theology*, s. v. "Apostle," by D. Muller.

[36]*Expository Dictionary*, s. v. "Evangelist,"

Euangelistes

This term literally means a messenger of good news. It is compounded from *eu*, meaning well, and *angelos*, meaning a messenger. It denotes a preacher of the Gospel (Acts 21:8, Eph. 4:11).[37] The term evangelist is used three times in the New Testament (Acts 21:8, Eph. 4:11, and 2 Tim. 4:5). It refers to a preacher of the gospel, the good news.[38] The work of an evangelist is to proclaim or announce good tidings, and therefore he is a teacher of the Christian religion.

In Acts 21:8, Philip is designated as an evangelist, and this same term is used of Timothy in 2 Tim. 4:5.[39] The evangelist did the work of announcing the Good News. He had a roving ministry among the unconverted, and was an itinerant missionary. He pioneered as a missionary. His pioneering ministry, in some cases, overlapped with the work of an apostle, but he held a lower rank and authority than that of an apostle. It is also logical to see the evangelist doing the work of establishing converts and gathering them into a congregation. The evangelist does the work of evangelizing (evangelize), that is, he is a preacher of the Gospel (Acts 21:8, Eph, and 2 Tim.4:5). Due to this fact we see any messenger of the gospel (good news) as an evangelist. Our category would include both the people trained to do the work of an evangelist on full-time basis and Christians in general who are called to tell the world of the good news. We do not hereby deny the fact that some are called to do full-time work as evangelists.

Prophetes

The prophet is defined as one who speaks forth, or openly. He is a proclaimed of a divine message. The prophesying of New Testament prophets was both a preaching of the divine counsels of grace already accomplished, and the fore-telling of the purposes of God in

---

[37] Gingrich, *Shorter Lexicon*, 80.
[38] *Expository Dictionary*, s. v. "prophet,"
[39] Gingrich, *Shorter Lexicon*, 173.

the future. In the New Testament the term prophet is used of the old Testaments prophets in general, of John the Baptist, of prophets in the churches, of Christ as the afore-promised prophet, of two witnesses yet to be raised up for special purpose, of the Cretan poet Epimerizes, and the writings of prophets.[40]

John the Baptist is called a prophet in Matt. 11:9, 14:5, 21:26, Mark 11:32, Luke 1:76, 7:26, and 20:6. Jesus called a prophet in Matt. 13:57, 16:14, 21:11, Matt. 6:4, 8:28, Luke 4:24, 7:16, 9:8, 24:19 John 4:19, 6:14, 7:40, and 9:17. The term prophet can be generally used of people who proclaim a divine message, as in Matt. 13:57, 23:30, Luke 10:24, 11:49, 13:33, and Acts 7:52, 21:10, 1 cor. 12:28, Eph. 2:20, 3:5, and 4:11. It was also used of a Cretan poet.[41] The term prophet is used in five senses in the New Testament. First, the Old Testament usage of a mouth-piece of God; second, of John the Baptist (the radical prophet of judgment and repentance); third, of Jesus Christ, the prophet-messiah; fourth, of men who were specifically commissioned; and finally, of Christian prophets who possessed the gift of prophecy.[42]

We are of the opinion that the New Testament church had a group of people who were designated as prophets, who had a ministry of prophecy. In 1 Cor. 12:28, 29, and Eph. 4:11, the prophets were listed as next to the apostles in the ministry listing. The prophets were associated with the teachers in the church of Antioch (Acts 23:1). Their function was customarily a double prophetic ministry of proclamation and prediction. As preachers, they had the ministry of exhortation (Acts 15:32), edification, and consolation (1 Cor. 14:3). They preached the message of sin and salvation, wrath and grace (1 Cor. 14:24, 25). We see prophecy as revelation, or perception, of the truth of God, which the prophet expounds. Thus, the prophet

---

[40]*Dictionary of New Testament Theology*, s. v. "Prophet," by C. H. Peisker.

[41]*Expository Dictionary*, s. v. "Teacher, False Teachers,"

[42]Gingrich, *Shorter Lexicon*, 48.

proclaimed and expressed the inspired speech of God. The New Testament prophets gave a message which was in keeping with already written work.

Didaskalos

This term is generally rendered teacher or teachers.[43] In Rom. 2:20 and Heb. 5:12 it is used to mean teacher. In Matt.8:19, Mark 10:17, Luke 9:38, and John 3:10 it is used as a term of honor and respect. In Acts 13:1, 1 Cor. 12:28, and James 3:1 it is used of Christian teachers in the Christian church. Apart from the normal usage meaning teacher, it is used of a master (Rom. 2:20), and in some places it is used as an equivalent of rabbi (John 1:39).[44]

The term *didaskalos* occurs fifty-nine times in the New Testament, twelve times in Matthew and Mark, seventeen times in Luke, and nine times in John. It refers to Jesus as teacher forty-nine times, as in Mark 9:17, 38 Matt. 8:19, and Luke 10:25. It is used to refer to John the Baptist (Luke 3:9), Nicodemus (John 3:10), scribes (Luke 2:46), and to teachers of the church (Acts 13:1, 1 Cor. 12:28, Eph. 4:11, and James 3:1). The author of the two epistles to Timothy calls himself *didaskelos* (1 Tim. 2:7, 2 Tim. 1:11).[45]

We conclude that the early church had a teaching office, and it was one of the charismatic offices in the triad (1 cor.12:28: apostles-prophets-teachers). These men had the task of explained Christian faith to others (Eph. 4:11, Acts 13:1, and James 3:1). The teachers explained matters of Christian faith, as well as matters concerning the Christian ethical duty (Titus 2:3). We also see a probability for the teachers to have held the office of shepherds or pastors (pastor-teacher, Eph. 4:11), which suggests the oversight of a local congregation and duty of instruction.

---

[43]*Dictionary of New Testament Theology*, s. v. "Teach," by K. Wegenast.
[44]Ibid.
[45]Ibid.

Summary of the New Testament Concept of Servant Leadership

One aspect of leadership in the New Testament is that of servanthood (Matt. 20:25-28, 12, Luke 1:2, 2 Cor. 3:6, 1 Tim. 4:6, Eph. 4:12). The person who is a leader is a servant of the people he is leading.

Another important aspect of a New Testament leader is that he cannot separate from his position of leadership. Christian living is part and parcel of a leader. Christian living and Christian leadership should not be taken in isolation (1 Tim. 3:1-10, 4:6; 1 Thess. 2:8 and Titus 1:5-16). A Christian leader is what he is, including his commitment and confession of the Lord Jesus Christ as his Savior, his allowing the Holy Spirit to guide his own life, and also his guiding of activities of those he is leading. He acts from faith within and from vision as directed of God.

A third aspect of New Testament leadership is of nurture (91 Thesis. 2:7-8). It involves care, gentleness, and cherishing. This is the type of ministry that the Lord Jesus Christ commissioned Peter to hold (John 21:15-17). Leadership is the ministry of tending and shepherding.

A fourth aspect of New Testament leadership is that of example (John 13:15, 1 Thesis. 2:9, 1 Tim. 4: 7b). The challenge for the leader is to do as he says, (not to tell Christians 'do as I say, and not as I do'). This same principle applies even in ordinary and worldly life, seen in proverbs such as "Actions speak louder than words." The leader's life is to be an example of holiness, justice, and blamelessness (1 Tim. 3:1-13, and Titus 1:4-16).

A fifth aspect of New Testament leadership is that of fatherhood. This calls the leader to function as a father, especially in guiding and teaching (Eph. 6:4). This may even involve disciplining, which ought to be done in love (Eph. 6:4).

Leadership in the New Testament means sacrificing, self-denial, and sometimes even death (Matt. 19:16-30, Mk. 10:17-31). This sacrificing leadership is seen in the example of Christ Himself 9Matt. 23:10-12). Tradition holds that Peter was crucified, his head down, and Paul was killed in persecution under Nero in A.D. 64.[46] The apostles underwent persecution because they were leaders of the Christian church. Imprisonment and being beaten were normal for church leaders.[47]

Paul, in writing to Timothy, said, "To aspire to leadership is an honorable ambition" (1 Tim. 3:1). But this leadership also calls for swallowing the bitter pill. Today church leadership has been misinterpreted and misrepresented by a few who clamor for honor, because of the honor and prestige which is accrued to those in positions of Christian leadership. A writer once wrote, "that true greatness, true leadership is achieved not by reducing men to one's service, but in giving oneself in selfless service to them."[48] Leadership in the New Testament involves the possibility of drinking a bitter cup and experiencing a painful baptism of suffering (Matt. 20:22). Leadership is never without cost. The true spiritual leader is concerned infinitely more with the service he can render God and his fellow men than with the benefits and pleasure he can extract from them. He aims to put more life that he takes out of it.[49]

Finally, leadership in the New Testament means responsibility and accountability (Luke 12:42-48). This connotes that Jesus' idea of leadership is a serious business. The person who holds a position of leadership exercises a greater responsibility, and he will have to give an account to Christ for that responsibility. As the saying goes "the heavier the responsibility the more the accountability."

Leadership in the New Testament is service (*diakonia*). The emphasis of leadership is servant-hood, rather than the superior attitude portrayed by those who lead. The activity of serving stands in contrast to ruling or "lording over." Christian leadership, as faithful

---

[46] Zondervan Pictorrial Encylopedia of the Bible, 3d ed., s. v. "Peter, Simon," by B. Van Elderen.

[47] Ibid.

[48] J. Oswald Sanders, *Spiritual Leadership* (Chicago: Moody Press, 1967), 13.

[49] Ibid.

service to God, presupposes humility in the one serves inferior in contrast to pride.

Christian leading (being in service, or servant-hood) is not ruling. Ruling provokes those being led, who feel under pressure, or under an intensive strain with the authority. 'Bossing' or 'Lording it over' builds a wall of resistance in which those being led build an attitude of resisting anything that comes from a leader.

We conclude that the Law of the Kingdom of God is "Greatness by services." This means that "greatness" (if at all it can over come from being a slave or servant of Christ) is not self asserted, or arrogated, but freely conceded by others. Service should not point to a higher place of dignity (*protos*) but to a *duolos* position, a lower and humbling depth or servitude.

A Christian leader serves in a position of dependence, and his freedom is limited. He is responsible and answerable to God. He must work within the scope set for him by the written *logos* (word), and exercise *pathos* (care and concern) as he serves his fellow men. A Christian leader cannot be separated from his office, just as the Christian message cannot be separated from the messenger. He exercises great care in his *ethos* (behavior in life). The church has always needed ministers, and not masters. Church leaders are ministers of God's people.

CHAPTER TEN

An Exegetical Examination of Ephesians 4:1-16

Introduction

The book of Ephesians is divided into two sections. The first deals with the adoration of the church glorious which is founded in Christ Himself (chapter 1-3). The second deals with the description of the organic unity of church in the midst of diversity (chapter 4-6).

We will deal with this second section which emphasizes the dependence of Paul's ethical advice upon the preceding doctrinal statement of the first section. Paul emphasizes unity, not an external and mechanical unity, but an internal and organic unity. Paul is showing us that one must be a child of God before he can be a servant of God. Thus, Paul shows us that ethics follow theology. The unity of the church is possible only by virtue of the power of the indwelling Christ. Chapter 4:1-6 encourages a personal initiative or an individual expression. This then means that unity is for the purpose of being a blessing to one another so that the church can be built up and be a blessing to the world. The two main themes of this second section are growth and unity. For the church to grow, each believer must co-operate and contribute his or her best to the inner growth of the church. The unity of the church rooted and grounded in love and this is compatible with the variety of gifts, offices, and stations.[1] Here, we see the apostle Paul move from the doxology of the new society to the new standards which are expected of it. He turns from exposition to exhortation, from what God has done (in the indicative) to what they must do (in the imperative), from doctrine to duty, from mind-stretching theology to its down-to-earth, concrete implications in everyday living.[2]

Maintaining the Unity: 4:1-6

The conjunction "therefore" is used here to show that what the apostle is about to say depends on what is preceding, what he has already said. This conjunction divides chapters 1-3 and chapters 4-6 practice and behavior (4-6) are the result of the application of doctrine (1-3). Doctrine comes before fellowship.

The verb *erotao*, translated "I beseech", can also be rendered, "I ask, I request, I encourage, I comfort, I warn."[3] The apostle has a great concern for the Ephesians church. He has a deep interest and concern for their spirituals welfare. In 1:15-23 and 3:14-9, the apostle taught and prayed for them respectively. He now exhorts them. Intercession, instruction, and exhortation constitute a formidable trio of weapons in any Christian leader's armory. The "I" he uses here is an emphatic personal pronoun. The purpose is to show them his apostolic authority (prerogative), and his pastoral anxiety was still powerful and intact.

Paul was a "prisoner in the Lord." We see two things here: one, he was telling his readers that his relationship to the Lord was as close and tender as when he first visited them; and two, he was "in the Lord," which when used in the Pauline epistles (see Eph.

---

[1] John Eadie. *A commentary of the Greek Text of the Epistle of Paul to the Ephesians* (Grand Rapids, Michigan: Baker Book House, 1979),267.

[2] John R. W. Stott, *God's New Society - The Message of Ephesians* (Leicester, England: Inter-Varsity Press, 1979), 146.

[3] Arndt and Gingrich, *Lexicon*, 311-312.

1:1-2, Rom. 16:3, 8, 9) suggests "in the Lord's service." The apostle was therefore, 'a prisoner of Christ' and 'a prisoner for Christ.' Being in prison for Christ, he was paying a price for being faithful to the Lord as well as for being in the Lord's service. On basis of these, he had a right to be heard and heeded.

The apostle continues on, "walk-conduct yourselves as men worthy of your calling." He calls them to walk worthy of their vocation (4:1). The Greek verb (*peripateo*) 'to walk' means to follow a prescribed way or a fixed order.[4] The 'calling' is an appointment to a position of honor, honorary place, and function with God has entrusted the saints. Two major characteristics of the 'calling' (*klesis*) are oneness and holiness, which are aspects of new life.[5] Step-step they are to walk in a direction that corresponds to their call (the whole plan of salvation). The call is to know the grace of God in Christ, to be the children of God, and to serve Him as His 'dedicated one's and messengers of His gospel.[6] Now that they have learnt the doctrine, they must balance that with practice and conduct. The call involves the obligation to live in a manner that is in accordance with the Name of Him whose they are and whom they serve (2:2, 1:18), pleasing Him in all things (Phil. 1:29; Cor. 1:10). The honor of Christ must be involved in their daily lives. This principle is to guide in every situation.

4:2 list the three aspects of such a life. These are three vital virtues are for every Christian. The three nouns are *tapeinophrosune, prautes,* and *makrothumia*. They describe the worthy conduct. The word arrangement is, "with all humility and gentleness, with patience." The three admonitions are: be humble and gentle, be pride, self-confidence, and self-assertion. Christians are therefore bound to cultivate lowliness (humility) and meekness

---

[4]*Expository Dictionary* s. v. "Walk,"

[5]*Expository Dictionary* s. v. "Call, Calling, Called,".

[6]Francis Foulkes, *The Epistle of Paul to the Ephesians* (Grand Rapids, Michigan: William B. Eerdmans Publishing Company, 1963), 108.

(gentleness), and long suffering (patience). It is through these that the unity of the church is established and maintained. Our faith sets before us not our own greatness but the greatness of God. We are the strongest no less than the weakest, dependent on Him in all things.[7]

For the Greeks, humility was not a virtue and they left no room for it. To the Greek mind, humility was little less than a vice of nature. It was weak and mean-spirited. It was the temper of the slave. It was inconsistent with that self-respect which every true man owed to himself. The fullness of life as it was conceived by them, left no room for humility.[8]

Humility (Tapeinophrosune) Results in Service and Self-Sacrifice

Humility means gentleness, courtesy, considerateness.[9] The apostle enforces humility on the ground of the relation of man to man in the great human unity. Humility,

> "Lowliness of mind . . . which stands at the extreme distance haughtiness, arrogance, and conceit, and which is produced by a right view of ourselves, and of our relation to Christ and to that glory to which we are called . . . This modesty of the mind, says Chrysostom is the foundation of all virtue"[10]

Meekness (*prautes*) means mildness or gentleness of character.[11] The objective prays means disciplined and controlled. Meekness in connected with the spirit of submissiveness. One who is meek does not assert his own importance, or authority. His every instinct and

---

[7]Brook Foss, Westcott, *St. Paul's Epistle to the Ephesians* (Minneapolis, Mnnesota: Klock and Klock Christian Publishers, 1978), 28.

[8]J. Armingtage Robinson, *Commentary on Ephesians* (Grand Rapids, Michigan: Kregel Publications, 1979), 91.

[9]Gingrich, *Shorter Lexicon*, 166.

[10]Eadie, *A Commentary*, 268-269.

[11]Gingrich, *Shorter Lexicon*, 121.

every passion, every motion of his mind and heart, and tongue and desire is under the perfect control of God.

Others are considered first. He strives to be in harmony with God's will. Meekness is, "entire subduedness of temperament which strives to be in harmony with God's will . . . and in reference to men thinks with candour, suffers in self-composure and speaks in the soft answer which turns away wrath."[12]

Humility and meekness result in patience (*makrothumia*).[13] patience (long-suffering (*makrothumia*) means slowness in avenging wrong or retaliating when hurt by another (1 Col 13:4, Gal. 5:22, Col. 3:12, 2 Tim. 4:2).[14] Patience enables a man to bear with those who oppose him, or who in any way do him injustice.

The practical outworking of long-suffering is bearing, or forbearing one another, and is a divine quality (Rom. 2:4). This involves bearing with one another's weakness which offends or displeases. This call for a mutual tolerance without which no group of human beings can live together in peace. One who bears is not shaken up, but continues to keep himself erect and firm as the original usage implies.

Lowliness, meekness, and forbearance are only possible in love. Love is the only origin, sphere, and nutriment of all these virtues. Love is the basic attitude of seeking the highest good of others. Love is the crown and sum of all virtues. Love is the climax and comprehensive virtue of the new life in Christ. Love as used here emphasizes outgoingness, true and tender affection toward the brother, the neighbor, and the enemy. Love is a noble endeavor to benefit the other party and never harm him in any way.[15] Love is not an emotion or an ideal but a personal quality, and a personal relation of saints which specific, costly, and miraculous.

---

[12]Eadie, *A Commentary*, 269.

[13]Gingrich, *Shorter Lexicon*, 121.

[14]Expository Dictionary s. v. "Patience,"

[15]William Hendriksen, *Exposition of Ephesians*, (Grand Rapids, Michigan: Baker Book House, 1967), 1

The Greek verb rendered 'take pains' (being diligent to preserve the unity in verse 3) calls for a full effort of the whole man, involving his will, sentiment, reason, physical strength, and total attitude. The taking pain is continuative (present participle). The unity spoken of, already exist. It had already been given and was present. For this unity to continue they needed to put effort and prayer. The point of emphasis for 'take pains' is to preserve that unity and take great care to keep it. It is a reality of the spiritual world. The basis for the unity is the relationship to Christ. The unity is in the relationship to Christ. There is no unity separate from the person of Christ and apart from the work of redemption through His blood. External peace tends to guard the inner fellowship. Unity in the faith corresponds with unity in the Spirit by which we are animated. Oneness *(enotes)* in the spirit issues from oneness in faith and knowledge of Christ. Unity dwells with the church and results from the one spirit (the originating cause being in the genitive). Christians are guardians of that unity, which rests upon the oneness of God, and must therefore keep it safe from all disturbance and infraction. The Spirit under discussion cannot be the human spirit which is not stable or sure. The unity of the spirit must be referring to the Holy Spirit, who alone is stable and sure.

Unity is Preserved and Manifested in the Bond of Peace
The term bond can be rendered technically or metaphorically. Technically, bond is that which keeps together two different members by joining them.[16] Metaphorically, the bond is that which preserves the unity.[17] The bond as used here refers to that which preserves and holds all virtues together. Peace itself is the bond as seen in the use of the genitive of apposition or identity.[18] The preservation of peace

---

[16] Eadie, *A Commentary*, 272.
[17] Expository Dictionary, s. v. "Bond,"
[18] W. Roberson Nicoll, ed., *The Expositor's Greek Testament*, 5 vols., (Grand Rapids, Michegan: William B. Eerdmants publishing Con., 1980), vol.3, Ephesians, by S.D.F. Salmond, 321.

as a bond among church members realizes unity. Unity is promoted by peace (1 Cor. 14:33, 2 Cor. 13:11, Phil. 4:7, col. 3:15. 2 Theses. 3:16, 2 Tim. 2:22). Where there is strife there is disunity. Peace promotes perpetuation of unity which in turn promotes health and happiness of the church.

We can conclude that the outer becomes the symbol, and expressions of the inner. When believers universally and mutually recognize the image of Christ in one another instinctively in spite of differences, and feel themselves composing the one church of Christ, they will endeavor to keep the unity of the spirit in the bond of peace.[19]

Verses 4-6 give a positive statement which lacks a *gar* or a connecting participle. It gives the objective group or basis on which to practice the unity of verses 1-3. The one body (*soma*) is the whole fellowship of *believers*, the mystical body of Christ (Eph. 2:16, Rom. 12:5, 1 Cor. 10:17, 12:13, Col. 1:24). The *peuma* is the Holy Spirit who is in the church and in whom we are baptized into one body (Eph. 2:18, 1 Cor. 12:13).

To be in Christ transcends and surpasses any association or society which bases its unity on things of this world. In this description unity, and all those characteristics associated with it, are traced first to the Holy Spirit who entered into the hearts of the believers. It then goes back to the Lord Jesus whose vicarious sacrifice had made possible the gift of the spirit. Finally, it goes to God the Father, who had given His son and who, together with the son, was also the giver or sender of the spirit.[20]

The church is one, despite its many members and complex array of organs of different positions, functions, and honor. The church, no matter where it is situated, or in whatever age of the world it exists, no matter of what race, blood, or color are its members, or how various the tongues in which its services are presented, is one, and remains so, unaffected by distance or time, physical, intellectual, and social distinctions.

---

[19]Ibid.

[20]Hendriksen, *Exposition of Ephesians*, 185.

There is one body, and only one spirit, one living principle, no double consciousness, no dualism of intelligence, motive, and action. There should neither be rivalry of administration nor confliction claims. The gifts and graces conferred, whatever variety or aspect they may assume, are all from the 'one spirit' and have oneness of origin, design, and result.[21]

This one body is vitalized by one spirit and progressing towards the goal of one hope. This body depends for its existence upon one Lord, its divine Head to whom it is united by one faith and baptism. Its ultimate source of being is to be found in one God, the Father of all, supreme over all, operative through all, immanent in all.

The 'calling' is a genitive of possession, that is, it should read, 'in one hope belonging to your calling.' Their call had brought them into possession of this hope. The spirit dwells in them (Rom. 8:9), and all who posses the spirit have a common hope.

The 'one Lord' (verse 5) means that He is one Head of the body, and the giver of its one spirit. We embrace the one Lord with one faith, used in the objective sense.

Reliance on our Lord Christ and on His promises must be true and genuine trust by which we embrace the one Lord Jesus Christ. The subjective oneness is created and sustained by the unity of its object (body of truth).

There can only be one baptism (verse 5). Baptism is consecration to Christ and dedication to the one Lord, the one mode of initiating by the one spirit into the one body.[22] The outward sign of faith and the 'visible word' expressing the work of Christ was baptism. This sacrament is a sacrament of unity.[23]

The Unity is in the God and Father of all (verse 6)

The name God is used both absolutely and with defining terms to show the special Fatherhood of God in grace (Redemptive Father-

---

[21] Eadie, *A Commentary*, 273.
[22] Ibid., 275.
[23] Hendriksen, *Eposition of Ephesians*, 186-187.

hood). The clause, "who is over all, and through all, and in all," expresses a three-fold relation of the one God and Father to all who are His,

> First, the relation of transcending or sovereignty expressing the supremacy of absolute Godhead and Father-hood.(See also 1Cor. 8:6, 12:5,6 and Rom. 11:36) Second, that of immanence expressing the pervading, animating, controlling presence of that one God and Father. (Christians live in a God-Created, God-controlled, God-Sustained and God-Filled world.) And third, that of indwelling and expressing the constant abode of the one God and Father in the people by His spirit (God indwells the Christian, and He works His purpose through the Chrisian).[24]

He exercises control over all. He blesses all through Christ. He draws us all close to His heart in the spirit. We submit the view that wrong doctrine of the church which contradicts Eph. 4:4-6 is what causes the problems in the church today. Most of our troubles arise chiefly from the fact that we persistently start with ourselves. We are too subjective. What we have to do therefore is to see ourselves as members of the church of Christ. As we do so we shall be delivered from most of our trouble and trials in church today.

When we see church leaders or church members having problems in our churches today which cause divisions, sects, and such related problem, the stem is the failure of a clear understanding of the nature of the church. All barriers must be broken down to enhance a genuine fellowship because the many differences in the church all over the world are caused by superficial things, or by the selfish individualism of members. William Hendriksen wrote,

> Unity is not external and mechanical but internal and organic. It is not superimposed but by virtue of the power of the indwelling Christ, but proceeds from within the organism of the church. Those therefore, who in the ecumenical zeal are anxious to erase all denomina-

---

[24]Salmond, *Ephesians*, 323.

tional boundaries and to create a mammoth super-church can find no comfort here. On the other hand, neither those who exaggerate differences and even stand in the way of inter-ecclesiastical co-operation when this can be accomplished without sacrificing any real principle can find comfort in Ephesians.[25]

The church is spiritually one. Unity is to be exercised with the purpose of being a blessing to one another. Unity should be exercised to build up the church and thus be a blessing to the world. This calls both church leaders and their church members to co-operate, and each contributing his share to the inner growth of the church. Seen clearly here is the organic unity of the whole church.

Description of the Organic Unity amidst Diversity: 4:7-16
Unity is the starting point. Each Christian is given this grace, which is divine mercy. The apostle and the readers had experienced 'the grace'. It was given by God and by which God worked in them. This subjective grace works within and shows itself in the result (charisma) which is the gracious faculty or quality. God's gracious relation to all is a relation also to each other. This grace is both a privilege and a responsibility. Each is able to stand pledged to do his part toward the maintenance of unity. Christ, the giver, gives both the large measure to one and a smaller measure to another, but each gets from the same hand and with same purpose. There are as many gifts and tasks as there are personalities. But each is dependent on others. God has ordained variety and not uniformity, but unity is seen in diversity. Each is given a different gift (function) for the benefit of all. No one had all the gifts.

The recipient of any gift or gifts must recognize that it a gift and not a product of his own works. He must recognize that his gift is one among many, limited in extent. He must as well be eager to use it for the benefit of the entire body and thus to the glory of

---

[25]Hendriksen, *Exposition of Ephesians*, 181-182.

God.²⁶ The diversity secures the individual his true of responsibility and honor.²⁷

Gifts are bestowed (distributed) by the Lord Christ to His church. The contexts here of the gift of apostles, prophets, evangelists, pastors, and teachers are examples of gifts which are gift to the church. He fills all in all. He, the giver, fills His church with all gifts. He leaves nothing unvisited in His church because He is present, and He gives in an appropriate proportion.

A major issue in Eph. 4:11 is whether, "some shepherds and teachers," which is translated, "some pastors and teachers," express two distinct offices, or two characters of the same office. Much has been written on this, but conclusions differ, for example. For *didaskaloi*, teaching was the main characteristic, yet from the mode of discharging it, it might be called a pastorate.

The *didaskalos* in teaching did the duty of a *poimen*, for he fed with knowledge, and the *poi men* in guiding and governing prepared the flock for the nutriment of the *didaskalos* . . . the one office is honored appropriately with two appellations. It comprised government and instructions . . . ²⁸

Others concluded otherwise. For example,

> Use of "pastor" as a title for the congregation's leader derives substantially from the Geneva Bible which follows Calvin's sharp formal distinction between *poi men* (pastor) and *didaskalos* (teacher) on his commentary on Ephesians.²⁹

Our careful examination of this verse has made us lean to the conclusion that the pastors and teachers are a single group of ministers

---

²⁶Ibid., 188-189.
²⁷Robinson, *Commentary*, 95.
²⁸Eadie, *A Commentary*, 305-306.
²⁹*International Standard Bible Encyclopedia*, s. v. "Pastor," by W.R. Harris.

whose two characteristics are shown here (see 1 Pet. 5:2, Acts 20:28, Rom. 12:7). We choose this view due to the following reasons: one, the Greek wording shows that shepherds and teachers belong together. Two, the article, *taus* and me*n* is missing before teachers, that is, "some" is not repeated before teachers. Three, the gifts of pastors and teachers are not sharply distinguished from one another as those that proceed. Four, pastors and teachers differ from the preceding classes in being attached to particular churches. Finally, the pastors work is to guide the sheep of the flock (1 Tim. 3:2, Titus 1:9), but this is done in the context of teaching, therefore his ministry includes that of being a teacher.

The apostles, prophets, evangelists, pastors and teachers are specific gifts given by the Lord. The *autos* is emphatic, meaning 'he himself' 'he and no other.' [30] The 'giving' refers to the call of the church's Head, the point being the gift of Christ to the church in the form of certain men chosen by Him, and equipped by Him to do service toward the building up of His body and the bringing all its members to the measure of the stature of His fullness.[31] The primary concern for the apostle Paul here is the persons not the offices. Frances Francis Foulkes wrote,

> The church may appoint men to different work and functions, but unless they have the gifts from the spirit, and therefore are themselves the gifts to His church, their appointment is valueless. The expression also serves well to remind ministers that the gifts of the spirit are not for the enrichment of oneself but for the enrichment of the church.[32]

They are given in their diversity of functions for the varied and harmonious development of the church. The apostle Paul is thinking of the ministers of Christ according to their specific spiritual gifts and their work (see 1 Cor. 12:28 and Eph. 4:11). See the previous sur-

---

[30] Gingrich, *Shorter Lexicon*, 30
[31] Salmond, *Ephesians*, 329.
[32] Foulkers, *The Epistle*, 117.

vey of the terms apostles, prophets, evangelists, pastors, and teachers in chapter one.[33] The purpose of these spiritual gifts is stated in a sentence consisting of three clauses. The second clause depends on the equipping of God's people for the work in His service, and to the building up of His body, the church W.Robertson Nicoll wrote,

> Christ gave some men as apostles, some a prophets etc., with view to the full equipment of the saints for the work of ministration of or service they have each to do in order to the building up the body of Christ. The building up of the church is the great aim and final object.[34]

The ruling idea is that each member gets the gift of grace, and each has his part to do towards the up building of the church. This is the great object of Christ's bestowments.

A major issue in Eph. 4:12 pertains to the work of the leaders mentioned in inclusion or exclusion of a comma in the passage. One, the leaders are to equip the saints and then go ahead and do the works of service. Two, the leaders are to equip the saints, so that the saints will do the works of service. If a comma is put between the first two concepts, that is, after "saints," then the aristocratic clerics will have all the service for themselves. All the saints will benefit from the ministries, but only select ministers will carry out the work of service, that is, the work of building the body. This would be in contradiction to 1 Cor, 12:7, 11, Eph. 4:7, and Rom. 12:6-8, which teach that each of the saints is uniquely gifted for some work of service for the common welfare of the body, the church. Saints would tend to become beneficiary spectators. Lawrence Richards and Clyde Hoeldtke wrote, "this is just the problem with imposing an institutional form of organization on the church. That kind of structure places leaders in controlling rather than equipping

---

[33] See 13-30.
[34] Salmond, *Ephesians* 331.

roles."³⁵ A. Duane Litfin commented, "then healthiest congregations are those in which these 'leadership' acts are widely dispersed, with 'every joint supplying, according to the working of each individual part' (Eph. 4:16) that which each is designed to contribute.³⁶ This view discourages the participation of saints in the work of construction of the body, the church.

The second option is to omit the comma from between the two parts of verse 12. If this is done, then the ministers of verse 11, who Christ has given to the church as gifts, will do the work of equipping saints to carry out the works of service. Richards and Hoeldtke wrote:

> Gifted men given and placed by Christ in the body "to prepare God's people for works of service, so that the body of Christ may be built up we all reach unity in the faith and in the knowledge of the son of God and become mature" (Eph. 4:12-13)³⁷

And they also wrote,

> Ephesians 4 gives us a suggestive insight into the role of leaders in the body ... we can note that even these special persons have as their mission not "to minister" but to "prepare God's people" for their ministry. ³⁸

The minister's role is not doing the work of ministry on his own but to function as a facilitator to equip saints for the work of service. To do this must:

---

³⁵Lawrence O. Richards and Clyde Hoeldtke, *A Theology of Church Leadership*, (Grand Rapids, Michigan: Zondervan Publishing House, 1980), 37.

³⁶A. Duane Litfin, "*The Nature of the Pastral Role: The Leader as a Completer*", *Bibliotheca Sacra* 139 (January-March 1982): 61.

³⁷ Richards and Hoeldtke, *A Theology*, 45.

³⁸Ibid., 49.

> Understand the leadership requirements of the local church. Back task and maintenance behaviors ... have the senility to diagnose in his congregation which of these leadership requirements are and are not being met by members of the group ... be able to help members of the congregation step in and fulfill those leadership behaviors which are "equiped" to fulfill the needed leadership functions. However, a pastor must be willing to step into the breach to fulfill the needed leadership behaviors himself as a stopgap means of completing what is lacking in the group ... he must bring to all of this a selfless devotion to the welfare of the group.[39]

It is our conviction that over emphasis of the leader's role as that of "equipping" can lead us into some leadership confusion especially when we literally take the statement, "The pastor's goal is to work himself out of a job."[40]

A pastor or any church leader is a saint, and therefore a member of the congregation; he should exercise his own gifts in the service of Christ. To conclude we shall use Duane Litfin's implications,

> A pastor ought never to do anything in the congregation that someone else can (will) do ... the pastor's primary task is to equip the saints for the work of ministry, completing for his part only what is lacking ... the goal of involving enable others to become involved in the ministry... equipping others to provide leadership in the congregation is a mark of success in the pastorate, not failure.[41]

The ministry of the church is given to it for the perfection of the saints, that is, bringing the saints to a condition of fitness for the discharge of their functions in the body, be fitted for the work of ministry.[42] The word used is *diakonia*, used of menial service (see

---

[39] Litfin, "The Nature," 63.
[40] Ibid., 64.
[41] Ibid.
[42] Richards and Hoeldtke, *A Theology*, 92.

Luke 10:40, 17: 8, 22:26, and Acts 6:2) and of service in general. For more details on draconian see the word survey in chapter one[43]

The ministry (service) done by saints and for saints is for edifying of the body of Christ (see 1 cor. 16:15). *Oikodome* (building) is used here to show what the church is increased and build up, and its members edified as each member used his particular gifts to give spiritual service to his fellow-members and to the Head, Christ.[44]

The unity in view is oneness in faith, in Christ, and oneness also in the full experimental knowledge of Him (v. 13). The first goal must be unity in the faith. The second goal is unity in knowledge of son of God. The spiritual unity already exists in believers and it should be guarded. The state in which unity is lacking is the stage of immaturity. The state in which oneness in faith and knowledge is reached is the state of mature manhood in Christ (see 1 cor. 13:11). Maturity (fullness in Christ) involves unity. Christian is a possessive genitive, and the phrase means the fullness that belongs to Christ, the sum of the qualities which make Him what He is.[45] When we have faith in Him and know Him, oneness can be imaged in the church. This goal can be attained and we can be perfect (*teleois*). Meaning we can be in complete possession of the gifts and grace. We can grow out of individualism into the corporate onesness of the full-grown man.

They should no longer be immature children (*nepioi*, v. 14) characterized by instability, insecurity, isolated individualism, alarmism and imperfectness. They should no longer be in a state of being tossed about in the storm and being carried away by the distractive influence of false teachers. They should be turned from their course, since they can be carried away by *kubia*, meaning playing with deco (hence trickery or fraud), or by *panourgia*, meaning craftiness.[46]

---

[43]See 13-30.
[44]Robinson, *Commentary*, 102.
[45]Eadie, *A Commentary*, 13-314.
[46]*Expository Dictionary* s. v. "Sleight,"

They must act with all simplicity and straight forwardness, being ambassadors of the truth and speaking the truth (*aletheuo*, v. 15) keeping to the simple way of truth and love, they will grow in stability and spiritual maturity. Maturity belongs to the unity. The way of growth for the individual is that: he should learn more and more to line in part of a great whole and contribute his share towards the completeness of the corporate unity. In the consciousness of a larger life we lose ourselves, to find ourselves again, no longer isolated, and uncoordinated in the body of Christ.[47] Every part of life should find its centre, object, and goal in relation to Him and in union with Him. Growth and every activity of the members is under His direction and obedient to His control (see Eph. 1:22, 5:23).

Christ is the source from which the grace or power comes that makes it possible for us to grow. He is also the object, and goal to which our growth in its every stage must look and is to be directed. All growth in the body has its source in Christ, the Head. *Harmos* and *sunbibasomenon* (v. 16) give the sense of a functional unity which is only possible by the direction of the Head, Christ, Unity is realized through and in Christ. He alone unifies and controls the organism. These words are in the present tense, and therefore express an on-going process.

The body is fitly framed and knit together by means of joints, everyone of them in its own place and function. These are points of connection between member and member. They are paints of communication between the different parts, and the supply which comes from the Head. The growth is normal, harmonious, careful of the capacity, and suited to the service of each individual member of Christ's body. The object and end of the carrying on of growth is the completion of the body.

In summary of verses 7-16, we note that the church has a unity of the spirit and unity in variety. The variety is principle of growth by which the church, the body of Christ, is moving towards maturity.

---

[47]Ibid.

Summary of Ephesians 4:1-16

The conjunction "therefore" shows that what the apostle Paul is about to say depends on what was preceding. Before there is leader, there must be the church of Christ, which is to be led. Paul is showing us that one must be a child of God before he can become a servant of God. Salvation is the beginning. This is a fact that most forgotten: we appoint people into the ministry of the church because they know the Lord. The basis for ministry is knowing the one to be ministered to, that is, ministers must be people who know the Lord as their personal savior. In serving our fellow believers, we serve the Lord Himself.

Verses 1-6 emphasize the fact of unity. The basis of unity' is the knowledge of one Lord, and the indwelling of the same Holy spirit. Verses 2-3 emphasize the oneness and holiness, thus the apostle exhorts the leaders as well as the entire church to walk in the prescribed order which corresponds to their walk. The four virtues prescribed here are essential for every Christian leader. Humility, gentleness, patience, and forbearance. No church leader who falls short of any of these can be worthy of ministry which will be a light and salt to the world. Verses 4-6 describe the unity of the body of Christ, the church. The basis for this unity is the one hope that all Christians are called to, and they have one Lord, one faith, one baptism, and one Father. Each Christian leader has a duty to teach the people he is leading that they are one. It is our hope that a leader who does this will find it easy to minister to the people he is leading. Paul taught the Ephesians church, and every church leader is called to do likewise. We leaders blame our people for disunity and disharmony instead of blaming ourselves. We must teach them the truth of the work of God.

Verses 7-16 serve as a good purpose of exhortation to church leaders today. "To each [is] given" a gift or gifts. It does not read "to pastors is given "or "to leaders is given." It can be a failure for the leader to assume that he is the only one given all the gifts and therefore be a 'Jack of all trades' in the church. It is also dangerous for leaders to over estimate themselves, and fail to use God-given gifts for the benefits of the church. It is equally dangerous for leaders to have gifts, be discouraged, and do nothing. The other aspect which comes out clearly is that a church leader is called, chosen, appointed, and equipped by God. In turn he has a responsibility to equip those God has put under his care. They are to be doing the work and service under his direction. We also learn that a leader should guard the people he is leading from false teaching that they may lead a blind man, therefore a leader must be mature, and not characterized by instability, individualism, and imperfectness. A church leader is called to confess the truth and lead the people to maturity. A church leader should not pride himself when he sees growth because it is God who causes growth.

Modeling for Servant Leadership

CHAPTER ELEVEN

An Exegetical Examination of I Timothy 3: 1-16

Introduction

This passage may be entitled "the high moral standard require ment for Christian leaders." The apostle Paul gave the in structions to Timothy to advise him on the order and government in the administration of the church. Both of these come second to public worship. The apostle gave the qualifications of the office representatives of the church, or of true spiritual leaders.

The apostle Paul emphasizes the personal characteristics which ought to distinguish those who might hold office in the church. These characteristics are predominantly moral attributes. The apostle hereby shows that to render meaningful service in the church, spiritual and moral qualifications come first. The church is the upholder and the historical basis of truth, therefore God retrospectively required high moral standards of the ministers of the church.

1 Tim. 3:1-16 consists of three sections: first, the qualifications for overseers (vv. 1-7); second, the qualifications for deacons (vv. 8:13); and third, the apostle's reasons for conveying of these instructions (vv. 14:-16).

Standard Qualifications for Episkopos *3:1-7.*
The terms *"Episkopos"* and *"presbyteros"* were used for the same church officials. We see them as two designations but one office. We see them as an equivalent of pastor because they watched and

had oversight over souls (for a survey of the terms episkopos and "presbyteros see chapter one"[1]

The office of an overseer was desired and sought by the Christians. At this time when the apostle Paul was writing, this was an office of danger and hardship. The aspirant actually needed encouragement from the church membership. To hold this office mean sacrificing, and an aspirant needed the willingness to suffer innumerable hardships. These was danger of persecution from Jews and /or gentiles. Patrick Fairborn wrote,

> It is not a post of honor, or a position of influence but a work of active service, and brings one into a living fellowship with the pure and good. Seeking is not a carnal ambition but an aspiration of the heart.[2]

This was an office which may rightfully be desired by the believer. Two strong verbs depict the yearning for this office which is commanded by Paul. "*Erego*" means 'to reach out after,' and the middle voice employed here indicates that the subject is reaching after this object for himself.[3] Such a yearning is described by a second verb "*epithumeo*", meaning 'meaning 'to desire, to fix the ardor or passion upon a thing.[4] The work desire can then sound harmful and sinful when read in the light of our later conditions. The office should seek the man, not the man the office. But here it is used in the good sense of strong desire. This godly desire, if controlled by the Holy Spirit, may deepen into a sacred conviction. On the other hand, this does not sanction ambitious aims at any high ecclesiastical position. It is the office which is described as being excellent or noble, and

---

[1] See 13-30.

[2] Patrick Fairbairn, *Pastoral Epistles*, (Minneapolis, Minnesota: Klock and Klock Christian Publishers, 1980), 136.

[3] Arndt and Gingrich, *Lexicon*, 583.

[4] Homeer A. Kent, *The Pastoral Epestles*, (Chicago: Moody press, 1958), 123.

therefore worthwhile. Paul employs the adjective *"kalos"* which means good intrinsically and outwardly commendable, beneficial, and acceptable.[5] It is beneficial to the one possessing it and if properly exercised, it is appreciated by those who behold it.

In turning to the qualifications for this office of overseeing, the apostle Paul greatly stresses moral and spiritual qualities. The apostle also emphasizes two essential testimonies, namely, from insiders (church-members) and from outsiders, that is, those who are outside the church[6]. The apostle also placed a great importance on the qualification of the family-relationship.

In verse 2a, the apostle gives a general qualification for an overseer: he must be blameless. The adjective *"anepilembano"* is derived from *"lambano"*, 'to take hold of' and epi, 'upon' with the "alpha" privative which negates the quality.[7] Hence the word is compounded to mean "not to be taken hold upon,"[8] that is, an overseer (bishop) must be such a spotless character that no one can lay hold upon anything in his life which would be of such a nature as reproach upon the cause of the Lord Jesus. He presents to the world at large such a Christian life that he furnishes no grounds for accusation.[9] We do not hereby advocate perfectionism for bishops, but it is our conviction that overseers (bishops) must portray a mature Christian living which gives no occasion for public reproach. We are of the view that an overseer must be a male due to the fact that every adjective in this list is masculine and the name overseer is masculine.

Verses 2b-7 gives us the specific qualifications. These qualifications concern the person of the overseer. The first qualification is

---

[5] Arndt and Gingrich, *Lexicon*, 402.

[6] William Hendriksen, *Exposition of the Pastoral Epistles*, (Grand Rapid, Michigan: Baker Book House, 1957), 119.

[7] Gingrich, *Shorter Lexicon*, 116.

[8] Kent, *The Pastoral Epistles*, 125.

[9] Kenneth S. Wuest, *Wuest's Word Studies, 3 vols.*, (Grand Rapids, Michigan: William B. Eerdmans Publishing Company, 1973) 2:52-53.

moral in character: he must be the husband of one wife. These are five views to this one qualification. The first view is that the overseer is to consider himself as married to the church. The second view understands this passage as prohibiting polygamy. The third view holds that a bishop may marry once but prohibits all second marriages. The fourth view holds that only the married men be overseers and all unmarried are excluded from this office. The fifth view prohibits divorce or any infidelity in persons chosen to the office of overseership.[11] The Greek for "the husband of one wife" is mias(one), *gunaikos* (woman), *and andra* (man). This can best translated as, "a one-wife sort of a husband," or "a one-woman sort of a man." We take this meaning because the two nouns man and woman are without the definite article, and such construction emphasizes character or nature. Our view is that an overseer must be morally pure. He must in a restrictive sense be faithful to his one and only marriage partner. The bishop must keep to what is conventional for all married men, therefore our view (which is the fifth one in the listing) above agree with H.P. Liddon in that we find ourselves in disagreement with any church discipline which does not allow married clergy.[12]

The second categories of qualifications for the overseer (bishop) are mental qualifications. These involve his personal conduct and his personal habits. Firstly, he must be sober, (*nephalion*) which means "to be calm, dispassionate, and circumspect."[13] Etymologically this term means abstaining from wine entirely. This is the view held in the evangelical churches in East Africa, including the holiness movement "East African Revival. It cannot be forgotten that this word *nephalion* means temperate in use of wine (1 Tim. 3:2, 11

---

[11] Kent, *The Pastoral Epistles*, 126-130.
[12] H. P. Liddon, *Explanatory Analysis of St. Paul's First Epistle to Timothy*, (Minneapolis, Minnesota: Klock and Klock Christian Publishes, 1978), 28.
[13] Wuest, *Word Studies*, 2:55.

and Titus 2:2).[14] This text cannot be used to justify total abstention from wine. Metaphorically the term 'sober' is used to mean 'spiritual sobriety,' 'temperate,' 'calm,' and 'sober in judgment.' Some have taken this second view and have emphasized moderation as the key thought.[15] In the model of East African Revival, Christians who are saved are required to abstain from drinking alcohol, except wine at Holy Communion. The overseer must be vigilant in habit, wakeful, and opposed to any kind of excess.

Secondly, he must be sound-mind (sober-minded, *sophrona*).[16] This is an adjective. It means a quality of mind which is serious, earnest, and sound. The connotation of this term is sensibility. He must not engage in a behavior which will be offensive to others. He must not convey exaggerated images.[17] One author wrote,

> Failure of ministers has not been due unfaithfulness in duty, or inability topreach, but by exhibitions of ungoverned temper and specific acts of indiscretion. To safeguard against this, the minister must strive and pray for sanctified common sense.[18]

Thirdly, he must be orderly *(kosmion)*. This suggests being dignified and orderly. This adjective is a cognate of kosmeo, to arrange the kosmos, that is, world (orderly arrangement).[19] It refers to a life which is well ordered, the expression of well-ordered mind. This orderliness refers to structure of his sermons, and his habits in physical, moral, or mental area.[20] Others translate this as respectable

---

[14] Arndt and Gingrich, *Lexicon*, 540.
[15] Robert C. Anderson, *The Effective Pastor*, (Chicago: Moody Press, 1985), 7.
[16] Wuest, *Word Studies*, 2: 55.
[17] Anderson, *Effective*, 138.
[18] Fairbairn, *Pastoral Epistles*, 138.
[19] *Expository Dictionary* s. v. "World,"
[20] Kent, *The Pastoral Epistles*, 131.

(of good personality, modesty, modesty and decorum.[21] This calls for prioritizing, regularizing, planning, and organizing all activities.

Fourthly, he must be able to teach, *(didaktikon)*. He must be apt to teach. He must be given to, able to, and skilled in the imparting of knowledge to others. This refers to ability and willingness to teach as a moral quality,[22] to faithfully discharge the ministerial functions of exhortation, convincing, teacher on doctrines of faith, and feeding of the flock. This moral quality must be there. He must be able to instruct in all matters both private and public.

The apostle Paul continues on to give some personality qualifications in the area of a minister's attitude and influence upon other people. First, he must be given to hospitality (hospitable, *Philoxenon*). The work *xenos* meant a stranger or a foreigner, a guest-friend, and from a host who gives and the strangers receives and entertains. The word "*philo*" refers one who has liking for, and is fond of something.[23] The compounded word means "one who is fond of offering hospitality, or loving strangers."

The hospitality spoken of here found its occasion in the fact of the great Roman persecutions, where Christians were banished, and rendered homeless. There were also traveling preachers and teachers who were to be received and cared for by the bishop. There were hardly church buildings for worship, the bishop had to be a man who would be glad to open his home for this purpose. Persecution, poverty, widows, and orphans all called for a bishop who would exercise hospitality. The term *me* translated 'not' introduces freedom from four gross vices. This is negative term. The bishop had to be free from these because they come in daily life as he rubbed shoulders with Christians.

Firstly, he must 'not be given to wine" (*me paroinon*.). It is made up of *Para* (beside) and *oinon* (wine). The compounded

---

[21] Anderson, *Effective*, 7.
[22] Wuest, *Word Studies*, 2:56.
[23] Ibid., 55.

meaning is 'one who becomes quarrelsome after drinking.' Such become intoxicated and hence quarrelsome. Two views come in here. In one, total abstinences is advocated, "I am convinced that the apostle would have advised the servant of God that a good rule of the thumb was avoid the use of alcoholic beverage entirely."[24] As East African Revivalists we take the total abstinence view for Christian leaders but not for general church membership. The second view is that of allowing drinking and not over-indulgence to the point where a bishop becomes quarrelsome after drinking.[25] It is commonly accepted that drunkenness often leads to blows or to an impetuous and violent behavior.

Secondly, he should not be a striker, (*me plekten*). He should not be a bruiser, or one who is ready with a blow, a pugnacious, contentious, and quarrelsome person.[26] This word is derived from the verb "*plesso*", to strike. It denotes a quick-tempered individual who strikes back with his first when annoyed.[27]

Thirdly, he should be gentle, *epieike*. This is defined as gentle, kind, yielding, and tolerant.[28] The main ideas of this word are patience, forbearance, and yielded ness. A person of this kind will avoid much contention. He will stop injuring saints because they do not enjoy being domineered.

Fourthly, he should not be a brawler (*amachon*). He should not be a fighter. This adjective denotes that he should be a person who is not contentious, and not offensively aggressive. He must keep his temper control. He should not glory in a good argument and win the argument by devastating his opponent with words.[29]

Fifthly, he should not be a lover of money, (*aphilarguron*). This word is compounded etymologically from "*arguros*" (silver,

---

[24] Anderson, *Effective*, 10.
[25] Wuest, *Word Studies*, 2:56.
[26] Ibid.
[27] Kent, *The Pastoral Epistles*, 132.
[28] Gingrich, *Shorter Lexicon*, 74.
[29] Anderson, *Effective*, 12.

money) "*philia*" and the "*alpha*" privative. 'To love' used here to mean 'to be fond of.' The love of money is in here. He should not be fond of money. It is our view that few things are more fatal to the position of a church leader that perceptible fondness for worldly treasure (money). If the soul of a pastor is groveling in the dust and the love of worldly treasure holds him captive, both he and his mission will be despised:

The overseer should not have his attention fixed upon monetary rewards. How frequently has the church suffered in reputation as well as in spiritual growth through the covetousness of some of her leaders? Furthermore, the poverty of many Christian ministers still does not remove this temptation from them. The love of money often leads to other sins. He who wishes to become rich also wishes to become rich soon.[30]

The next qualification is a domestic qualification. The way in which a man controls his home reveals his capacity for any type of leadership whether in the church, in secular organization, or in government. An overseer is to rule his house. The word is *proistemi* which means 'to superintend or beat the head of, or to preside over.'[31] His children are to *hupotage*, meaning that they are to live in obedience and subjection." [32] What we see as the issue here is management and control. The administrative ability required to cause a home to function smoothly will also be required in the church. A minister's character is portrayed and seen to best advantage in the framework of his own family. His ability to preside will best be revealed in a well-ordered household where the children are in habitual subjection.[33] Deficiency in matters at home (incompetence to manage his own children) disqualifies a man from serving in a ruling capacity in the church. The apostle Paul is showing us that ill-trained,

---

[30] Kent, *The Pastoral Epistles,* 133.
[31] Gingrich, *Shorter Lexicon,* 168.
[32] *Expository Dictionary* s. v. "Strider,"
[33] D. Edmond Hiebert, *First Timothy* (Chicago: Moody press, 1957), 66-67.

bad children reflect on the pastor, not merely because they are hurtful examples to the children of the members of the church, but still more because they show the father is incompetent for the office.[34] God often teaches us more by our domestic experiences than we can learn by independent speculations, however spiritual they may be seen. The submission of children tests the capacity for leading. Respect and dignity portrays the family relationship to their father, and their characteristics will entitle their father to reverence (respect), dignity, gravity, majesty, he must manage his household well (*kalos*), that is, beautiful, finely, and excellently.[35]

In relation to the church, the overseer must not be a 'novice' (*neophutos*). This is made up of "*neos*" (new) and "*phuo*" (to spring up).[36] It means 'newly planted.' In the spiritual sense it is used here to refer to a new convert. The overseer must not be a new convert. Maturity in the Christian faith is essential. His intelligence and solidity of character need to be already proved. The elevation of a "*neophutos*" inflates him with pride (*tuphoo*). The term "*tuphoo*" means to raise a smoke, to emit smoke, and hence "to blind with pride." It describes a person who is in a beclouded or stupid state of mind as the result of pride[37].

If such conceit occurs, the judgment which was meted out to Satan, (Satan is under condemnation because of his original sin of rebellion against God which was motivated by pride) may happen also to the novice. The sudden elevation of a novice may build conceit and confusion which has been a tendency for carrying such off his feet, and thereby become prey for the evil. This attendant warning tells the church that there are temptations and perils peculiar to ministry, so men should not be haste to enter it nor should others seek to push them prematurely.[38]

---

[34]Ibid., 67.
[35]Wuest, *Word Studies*, 2:57-58.
[36]Ibid., 58.
[37]Ibid.
[38]Fairbairn, *Pastoral Epistles,* 144.

In daily life, the overseer rubs shoulders with people outside the church, both Jews and the heathen public, so the overseer must have a good reputation from the time of his conversion. The Greek words are "*murturian kalen*", and are translated "an excellent testimony" from "those without." "Those without" here refers to the non-Christian world in the midst of which saints live.[39] Their testimony might usefully balance or correct that of the church. The public opinion not be disregarded or defied because this might bring discredit on one's self, on the church, and catch us in the devil's snare. The reproach (*oneidismon*) may refer to the accusation which men might make against him.[40] The snare of the devil *(pagida tou diatolou)* A. kent quoted white:

> St. Paul's attitude towards "them are without" is one of the many proofs of his sanity of judgment. On the other hand, they are emphatically outside the church; they have no "*locus standi*" in it, no right to interfere . . . their moral instincts are sound and their moral judgments worthy of respect . . . there is something blameworthy in a man's character if the consensus of outside opinion be unfavorable to him, no matter how much he may be admired and respected by his own party.[41]

Such testimony is essential so that those outside do not think lightly about the Christian church or mar the success of the ministry of the overseer.

Standard Qualifications for the Diakonos 3:8-13

The deacons was a server , (see Acts 5:6, 10). For a survey of "*diakonia, diakonos,* and *diakoneo* look at Chapter Nine of this

---

[39] Wuest, *Word Studies*, 2: 57-58.
[40] Gingrich, *Shorter Lexicon*, 139.
[41] Kent, *Pastoral Epistles*, 135-136.

book.[42] See also Rom 12:7, 1 cor. 12"28, and Phil. 1:1. From the title given to the office (*diakonos*), and from the cognate verb employed in verse 10 (*diakoneitosan*), it is our conclusion that the nature of the office is ministering or serving. It is also our view that these church leaders were charged with the temporal welfare of the local church (at the time the apostle Paul was writing). We take the view that the deacons were distributors of church funds had a danger of making illicit gains on the money which passed through their hands.

The apostle Paul lists their qualifications, and the first deals with their personal character. They were to be dignified *(semnous)*. This term is positive, and means worthy of respect, stately, and dignified.[43] It denotes a seriousness of mind and character as well as reverence. This service done to the whole congregation (local church) is to be undertaken with a sense of gravity (seriousness) but this does not mean that they could be austere or unbending in the carrying out of such work. Secondly, he names three negative qualifications, which, if present, would disqualify the deacon. He should not be double tongued (*me dialogus*) meaning, "saying one thing and meaning another, and making different representations to different people about the same thing."[44]

The temptation of such a person who would be in constant visitation would be to speak of the same matter in different tones and manner. He would be giving conflicting tales and would spread havoc in a short time. The main idea here is that a deacon must be one who knows how to bridle his tongue. He should not be holding to much wine, that is, not to hold toward, not apply one's self to, not to attach one's self to much wine. The context indicates that wine was a common beverage. The problem was that of abusing the us-

---

[42]See 77-94.
[43]Kent, *Pastoral Epistles,* 137.
[44]Wuest, *Word Studies*, 2:59.

age of wine. He must not be holding his interests and attention toward wine.

The social stigma, tremendous social evils and crime, and as one of the major causes of family breakdowns, and problems of infertility and role taking, and alcoholism that accompany drinking today did not attach themselves to the use of wine in homes of Paul's day. We see the dangers of drinking more clearly and hold to the ethics of "no wine at all." We, in the East African Revival Movement, therefore, hold to no wine at all for deacons, priests, bishops and other church leaders, and if possible for all Christians. But this view here does not come from this text, rather, it is a biased Colonial imposition. We cannot be dogmatic about this view, therefore it is open linguistically for interpretation, misrepresentation and misreading. But the familial, biological and social effects of alcohol abuse cannot be refuted.

The Christian servant and leader should not be shamefully greedy of gain. The words in Greek are *me aischorkerdeis*. *Aischorkordes* is compounded from *aischros* (disgraceful) and *credos* (gain). The words "not greedy of gain" are used for a deacon involved the distribution of alms to the needy, and is dishonest in that distribution. Charles R. Erdman says, "Judas was not the last treasurer who betrayed his Lord for a few pieces of silver."[45] Many who have access to church finances have had an opportunity to act dishonestly. The *kerdos* (gain) becomes *aishoron* (disgraceful), when a man makes the acquisition of it his prime object, rather than the glory of God.[46]

The apostle Paul turns to the possession of vital spiritual life as a qualification for a deacon. He or she must be known as "holding the mystery of the faith." Mystery (*musterion*) has the idea of something previously hidden (unknown) but is now revealed (divinely to

---

[45]Kent, *The Pastoral Epistles*, 139.
[46]White, *1 and 2 Timothy and Titus*, 4:115.

the believer by the illumination of the Holy Spirit).[47] The genitive tense, *tes pisteos* of the "faith mystery" is a descriptive or defining genitive which explains what this mystery is. The mystery is the body of truth which comprises Christian faith. These great truths of the faith are to be properly employed in daily life. To hold the mystery of the faith in a pure conscience is to live in the light of Christian church. A deacon must be known as holding a pure conscience which as an indication or a pure life. Christian faith and daily life are intimately related, and we can conclude by saying that the, "practical Christian life comes from theoretical understanding of the work of God." See Rom. 16:25, Eph. 1:9, and Eph. 3:4.

The apostle Paul now introduces the idea of proving the appointees by "these also," implying that the bishops (previously referred to) as well as deacons (now under discussion) must be proved before being appointed. Christian experience must be tested in candidates before appointment. The word "proved" is *dokimazesthosan*. This is a verb and is a present imperative. It means "to be put to the test for the purpose of approving, and having met the test to be approved."[48] This refers to a constant observing or testing, so that when deacons are needed, qualified ones may be nominated. This does not mean a formal test or formal examination. This shows then that persons who have been under observation by the church for an adequate length of time can be termed "un-accused" or "blameless" (*anegkletoi*) if nothing disqualifying has appeared. The participle notes is a conditional one, meaning they are appointed because they are uncaused.

There are different views on the proper translation of the word *gune*, "wives" and is best translated "women." The problem is whether this refers to "wives of deacons" or "to an established office of deaconess." One author gave the following reasons for the second reference. First, "even so" (*hosautos*) is used in introduc-

---

[47]Kent, *The Pastoral Epistles*, 139.
[48]Wuest, *Word Studies,* 2:60.

ing a second or third in a series. Second, there is no possessive pronoun which would be needed in Greek to refer to wives. Third, the following four qualifications have variations from those of deacons. Fourth, this section is dealing wholly with church officials.[49] Another author gave the following to support the view of a separate office of deaconess. Firstly there were deaconesses in the first century church (Phoibe in Rom.16:1). Secondly, the structure of the passage indicates a transition to another class. Thirdly, the term "wives" is the simple word "woman" (*gunaikos*), the general term "*gune* " was used and the reader is left to infer "woman deacon." Fourthly, this cannot refer to all Woman in church because the context deals with officials of the church. Fifthly, this cannot be limited to the wives of deacons because there is no grammatical connection between verses 11 and verse 8-10.[50]

In our opinion, a separate office of deaconess has a stronger case. The qualifications for the female deacons are listed here in verse 11. They must be grave (*semnos*). Meaning they must be serious with their work, and must do their work with dignity. With gravity and dignity they invite the reverence of others. They must be not slanderers *(me diabolous)*. *Ho diabolos* is substantively used for the devil, the chief slander of God and the people of God. *Diabolous* comes from *diabollo* which means, "to throw over or across, to traduce, calumniate, slander, accuse, defame."[51] The deaconess must not partake of this characteristic of the devil. She must avoid using improper speech. The deaconess must be sober (*nephalion*), meaning "to be calm, dispassionate, circumspect."[52] For more details see the above on verse 2. The deaconess should be faithful in all things (*pistas en passin*). Faithful is used in the sense of fidelity. She must be true to the trust imposed in her. Faithfulness entails trust-worthiness in ecclesiastical duties, and in do-

---

[49]*Expository Dictionary*, s. v. "Woman,"
[50]Wurst, *Word Studies,* 2:61.
[51]Kent, *The Pastoral Epitles*, 140-141.
[52]Arndt and Gingrich, *Lexicon*, 181.

mestic affairs such as faithfulness to her husband, to her family, to Christ, and to the church.

In verse 12, the apostle Paul gives the domestic qualification of deacons. They are to be married only once and one wife sort of husband as well as being faithful to that one and only wife. They must rule their children and household in a commendable manner. The word "ruling" is *proistemi*," "to be over, to superintend, to preside, to preside over."[53] The ability of a deacon to preside will best be revealed in a well ordered household where the children are habitual subjection. The habitual subjection denotes that the children see the dignity of their father and thereby obey him.

The deacons who do their work well obtain a good a standing (v.13). One author said that this implied a promotion because the episcopes were naturally drawn from the ranks of the deacons, the diaconate was a probation time. In the course of which the personal moral qualifications for the episcope might be acquired.[54] The word perspire (acquire or obtain) and the word bathmon (degree-a step in order, possible apromotion.[55] The interpretation of these verses has differed due to the understanding of the word bathmos which can mean a step, rung, base or degree in rank, standing. Some as above take it to mean advance in ecclesiastical office (this happens but it is not always the case).[56] We are of the view that this refers to a good standing in the eyes of God and of men because of serving well. One concludes, "He is achieving a respected reputation in the church. He is also laying up treasures in heaven, so that in the day of Christ he will have a good standing when rewards are distributed."[57]

When a deacon serves well he also gains *paresis* (boldness), which primarily means "free and bold speaking or speaking out every word."[58] The dominant idea is boldness and confidence, "an

---

[53] Gingrich, *Shorter Lexicon*, 132.
[54] Wuest, *Word Studies*, 2:61-62.
[55] White, *1 and 2 Timothy and Titus*, 4:116.
[56] Wuest, *Word Studies*, 2:62.
[57] *Expository Dictionary* s. v. "Degree,"
[58] Kent, *The Pastoral Epistles*, 143.

assured position and blameless reputation in the church with a pure conscience, would assure boldness of speech and of altitude in the Christian community and elsewhere."[59] The deacon is thus bold and confident to approach God in prayer because he knows that there is no sin or carelessness in spiritual matters.

Verses 14 and 15 tell us why the apostle Paul gave to Timothy these instructions concerning the officers of the local church, their duties and qualifications, and matters of church discipline. Timothy needed to know how he should behave himself and how the members of the church should conduct themselves. Timothy, Paul's official representative, has to see that the affairs in the church at Ephesus were organized and carried on properly. Timothy had to know these regulations in order to effect them in the church.

The term *ecclesia* (church) comes from the verb equaled meaning "to call out of." This word is used of an assembly summoned for purposes of deliberation (Acts 19:39), of an assembly of Israel (Judges 21:8. 1 chronicles 29:1), an assembly summoned for sacred purposes (Deut. 31:30, Joshua 8:35), and of the whole body of Christians, who are in covenant relationship with Christ (Matt. 16:18, 1 cor. 12:28, Eph. 1:22, 3:23, Phil. 3:6, col. 1:18, 24).[60] The church is a composition of a body of called out people, called by the sovereign grace of God into salvation. The church, designated "God's house" (*oikoi theou*) is the spiritual house of believers built upon Christ, the great foundation, in which house God dwells.

The church upholds in the word, the truth which God has revealed to men. The church is the pillar and ground of truth. The word "ground" is *hedraioma* (a stay, a prop-firm, stable). The words, "pillar" and "ground" are in apposition to the word church. They indicate the function of the church in relation to the gospel (the truth). The pillar holds up and supports it. The idea here is that the church is the pillar, and the prop or support of the truth. The church stands

---

[59] Wuest, *Word Studies*, 2:62.
[60] Arndt and Gingrich, *Lexicon*, 240-241.

from age to age upholding the truth before men. In upholding the truth it catches the eyes of men.

Summary of 1 Tim. 3:1-16

The nature of Christian leadership calls for high spiritual and moral qualifications. Leadership is not a high position of office but a life of high God-pleasing characteristics. For leadership to be effective, the catalogue of qualifications must be regarded with all necessary seriousness. One author on reading 1 Tim. 3:1-16, commented, "Spiritual standards to not change from generation to generation, but remain the same in the space age as at the birth of the church. None of these qualities here enjoined by Paul are optional extras, but indispensable requirements."[61] Spiritual qualification involves the whole personality, therefore these qualifications have divided into social, moral, mental personality, domestic, and maturity categories.[62]

The following categories of qualifications for Christian leaders are discussed in 1 Tim. 3:1-16,

- One, testimonies must be sought from church members and from those from outside the church.
- Two, the general qualifications are being blameless (a character with not grounds of accusation).
- Three, character specifics involve personal morality, mental sobriety, sensibility, dignity and order, and the ability to teach.
- Four, qualifications that relate to leader's attitude to other people are: lover of people, not given to wine which leads to violent behavior, not quick-tempered, not contentious, and not fond of money.
- Five, the domestic qualifications concern his ability to administer his household, respect and dignity shown by children, all of which show good management which is needed in the church.

---

[61] Sanders, *Spiritual Leadership*, 29
[62] Ibid., 29-37.

- Last, but in no way least, is the need for maturity in Christian life. Intelligence and solidity of character must be seen or proved before one is appointed into positions of leadership.

The emphasis of this passage is that a leader is to be highly scrutinized before being placed into a church leadership position. A Christian leader who falls short of these qualifications automatically disqualifies himself or herself. This check list is for personal use for every Christian leader. The church of Christ throughout the world is bound by these qualifying qualities of order and discipline.

CHAPTER TWELVE

An Exegetical Examination of Titus 1:1-16

Introduction

The passage under discussion is in a pastoral letter written by the apostle Paul, and was intended to convey through Titus a message to the church. Titus was a leader left in the church in Crete and is mentioned in Galatians 2:1-3, 2 Corinthians 3:13, 7-8; 12:18, and 2 Timothy 4:10. He was a servant of Christ, known as a man of exceptional ability which was seen in his collecting of money in a divided church for the poor. This is the type who was left by Paul in Crete to carry out the organizational work of the church.

Titus 1:1-16 centers itself on the administration of the church. Verses 1-4 form the salutation. In this salutation apostleship and services of Paul are discussed. Verses 5-9 concern the selection and qualification of elders in church administration. Verses 10-16 explain why it is necessary to have highly qualified elders to do proper administration of the church. The other aspect that comes out of this section is that of discipline. There were disreputable men in Crete who needed to be sternly rebuked. The book of Titus stresses the idea that sound doctrine goes hand in hand with the life of sanctification and the doing of good works.[1] The apostle wrote this letter to give directions of church administration which can promote spiritual sanctification.

---

[1] Hendriksen, *Exposition of the Pastoral Epistles*, 339.

The Personal Characteristics of Paul (1:1-4)

Paul's position of service and apostleship is given by two designations, (see Rom.1:1, Phil. 1:1). See also James 1:1, and 2 Peter 1:1. Paul is a bond-servant of God and an apostle of Jesus Christ. The usage of dulls as used here has brought some interpretative problems because it should be rendered slave or servant. The emphasis of Paul as God's slave *(doulos)* or servant is that of "one who gives himself up wholly to another's will," not just a worker.[2] For a survey of *doulos* see New Testament vocabulary for leadership in chapter one.[3]

This noteworthy variation is a mark of genuineness.[4] Paul is Jesus' apostle, that is, he is exercising the bond of service by carrying out the commission that Christ had given him. Paul serves Christ to the disregard of his own interests and this causes him to live a life of self-sacrifice. Paul's ministry of apostleship can be measured in accord with *(kata)*, or in harmony with, the faith which God's elect can possess. The believers' faith *(pistin)* and full knowledge of truth *(epignosin asthenias)* could be used as yardstick to measure Paul's ministry.[5] Paul's apostleship corresponds to, is fitting, and is congruous with, the precise and experiential knowledge, of truth.

Paul's service and apostleship are exercised in the interest of God's elect, and rest upon (upon the basis of) a hope of life eternal. Hope here is viewed as a kind of energizing cause of Paul's apostolic ministry and of the elects' complete devotion to God. Faithfulness in the performance of his own task and incentive for holy living of believers are caused by the "hope for life everlasting," The work hope is used here to refer to an earnest yeaning, confident expectation, and patient waiting for life everlasting. Salvation in its fullest

---

[2]Fairbairn, *Pastoral Epistles*, 216.
[3]As above.
[4]Hendriksen, *Exposition of the Pastoral Epistles*, 341.
[5]Kent, *The Pastoral Epistles*, 218.

development is expressed by the word "hope" (see John 17:24, Rom. 8:25).[6]

Instruction Concerning Administration of the Church 1:5-16

Selection and qualification of elders in church Administration (1:5-9)
The apostle Paul on leaving Titus behind in Crete had given him an oral command, and here again repeats it:

> The command now given to Titus in writing was to put in order the administrative affairs of the church on the Island. Paul had began this work personally, and now Titus is urged to carry it further (prefix epe, "in addition," attached to the verb "put in order").[7]

To accomplish this command, Titus had to arrange the selection of elders. The verb used here is *kathistemi* and it means "to set down, establish, arrange."[8] It is used here to refer "to appoint one to administer an office."[9] Titus was to appoint (*diatasso*) meaning "to prescribe, give a charge".[10] This verb does not tell Titus how the selection would be made (see Acts 14:23 and 2 cor. 8:19). He had the duty of appointing a number of *prebyteroi*, that is, elderly men of approved Christian reputation. (See the New Testament vocabulary for leadership survey section for a survey of the term presbyteros.[11] Many biblical scholars hold that eldership was not a distinct office, 'elders are synonymous with overseers (bishops).

---

[6]Wuest, *Word Studies*, 2:183.
[7]Kent, *The Pastoral Epistles*, 218.
[8]*Expository Dictionary* s. v. "set,"
[9]M. Blaiklock, *The Pastoral Epistles*, (Grand, Rapids, Michigan: Zondervan Publishing House, 1972), 75.
[10]Arndt and Gingrich, *Lexicon*, 188.
[11]As Above.

The former term connotes their dignity, and the latter their function."[12] Paul's purpose in leaving Titus temporarily in Crete was for him to appoint elders in each city. The apostle now (in verses 6-9) gives the qualifications which Titus must look into the selection of elders. Let us briefly discuss these qualifications.

The General Qualification of an "Unaccused" Elder.
It was a difficult matter in this island of Crete to get a man of irreproachable character, and of unquestionable integrity. The apostle knew this, but he was sure there were people of this kind in the church in Crete, with these marks for leadership. The Cretins had a poor reputation in the ancient world, but Titus duty of leadership was to stand firm against the defects of the Cretan character.[13] The characteristics of Crete will be explained below. Paul relates firm that a man to be selected for eldership be of deservedly high reputation. The adjective "unaccused" *(anegkletos)* is derived from *kaleo* (call), *en* (in), and the alpha privative (not), and means "one who is not called in question or called to account".[14] He must have lived an exemplary life with no occasion to call him to account or bring a charge against him. He must be a male who cannot be successfully accused on any of the matter. This strict qualification is needed because of the elder's nature of ministry, as a steward of God's property, the church.

The Family Qualifications of an Elder
The elder must be a husband of one wife (for this family virtue see the exegesis of 1 Tim. 3:2 above). He should have believing children. Unbelieving children could be a great handicap to the ministry of an elder. He must not have unruly children (*asotia*, meaning an abandoned, dissolute life, or profligacy),[15] His children must not be

---

[12] Wuest, *Word Studies*, 2:184.
[13] Ibid.
[14] Arndt and Gingrich, *Lexicon*, 63

accused of rioting, disparity, or rebellion. They must not be *anupotaktos*, meaning that they "cannot be subjected to control."[16] Such children can be a source of embarrassment to their father because of their unrighteous living. They must be children who can be brought to subjection.

Personality Qualifications of an Elder

He should not be self-pleasing (*me authade*). This adjective is made up from *hedomai*, meaning "to enjoy one's self, take one's pleasure", and *autos*, meaning "self." When compounded the word means "self-pleasing, self-willed, arrogant."[17] He must not be a man who disregards others. He should not be "a soon angry" (*me orgilon*). *Orgilon* means "prone to anger, irascible." He must not be prone to anger. The *orgilos* is "one who has not his passion of anger under control."[18] He must be not be a man prone to anger but a man who keeps his anger under control.

He must not be a lover of wine, and not a striker (see above notes on 1 Tim. 3:3). He must not be given to filthy lucre (not greedy of gain, see above 1 Tim. 3:8).

He must be hospitable, a lover of hospitality (see above on 1 Tim. 3:2) He must be a lover of goodness (*philagathon*), meaning "loving what is good."[19] He should be devoted to all that which is good and beneficial. He should be sensible (sober or sound-and good things.

---

[15] Wuest, *Word Studies*, 2:184.

[16] W. Robertson Nicoll, ed. *The Expositor's Greek Testament, 5 vols*, (Grand Rapids, Michigan: William B. Eerdmans Publishing Con., 1980), vol. 4 1 and 2 Timothy and Titus by New Port J. D. White, 187.

[17] Ibid.

[18] Gingrich, *Shorter Lexicon*, 49.

[19] Arndt and Gingrich, *Lexicon*, 194.

Spiritual and Moral Qualifications of an Elder

The elder should be righteous *(dikainon)*. His conduct must be upright, just, law-abiding, honest, and fair.[20] He must be conforming to the laws of God and man, and living according to them. The legal aspect emphasizes law abiding. The religious aspect emphasizes not violating the sovereignty of God and keeping His laws.[21] Being a legal term, such a verdict is pronounced by God, the divine judge, but these qualities can be seen by man's eyes.

The elder should be holy *(hosion)*, meaning unpolluted. When it is used men, it refers to devout, pious men who are pleasing to God.[22] The conduct of an elder must be true to his moral and religious obligation. The elder is called to observe the true and established ordinances of the Lord.

The elder should be self-controlled and temperate, translated from *egkrate*. This word originally meant "having power over, possessed of." It is used here to mean "keeping in hand, controlling."[23] Self-controlled refers to being disciplined also. He must have power over, hold in check, and be restrained, especially in regard to sensual appetites (most of the other qualifications are already discussed).

He should be one holding fast *antecho,* meaning holding firmly to). This also suggests withstanding opposition. He should hold firmly "in accord with the doctrine." The "faithful word" means "the trustworthy, reliable word". This word is worthy of trust because it is reliable.[24] He must hold to his God's word, which is in accordance to the recognized body of Christian truth which is the apostolic teaching (Acts 2:42). Two reasons are given for this qualification. Firstly, to be able to encourage and exhort *(parakelein,* meaning "beg of you, please") believers in the healthful teaching of

---

[20]Ibid., 589.
[21]Wuest, *Word Studies*, 2:185.
[22]Ibid.
[23]Ibid.
[24]White, *1 and 2 Timothy and Titus*, 188

the true doctrine. He must be able to exhort in sound teaching.[25] By this he will be able to protect his people from error and from false teachers, "The shepherd must be able to tend the sheep, and to drive away wolves."[26] Secondly, to be able to convince the "ones" contradicting. Convince is *elegcho* meaning "to convict so as to bring forth convict in or confession." The "contradiction" were people who were spreading against." He needs to be able to refute those who oppose the sound doctrine with diseased teachings of legalism and error, especially against machinations and Judaism in the church.

Presence of False Teachers Calls for Proper Administration of the Church (1:10-16)

Paul's thought in verses 10-16 can be paraphrased as:

> I have just mentioned rebuke as a necessary element in a presbyter's teaching. This is especially needful in dealing with Cretan heretics, in whom the Jewish strain is disagreeably prominent. Alike in their new-fangled philosophy of purity, and in their pretensions to orthodoxy, they ring false. Purity of life can only spring from a pure mind; and knowledge is alleged in vain, if it is contradicted by practice.[27]

It was necessary to have highly qualified elders for spiritual offices because of the type of men in Crete. There was not one but many such unruly ones,

> "The persons spoken of here were Christian Jews . . . they were at least nominally Christians as implied by the epithet 'unruly.' We cannot call those persons "unruly" on whose obedience we have no claim.[28]

---

[25]Ibid.
[26]Ibid.
[27]Ibid., 189.
[28]Ibid.

These men were uncontrolled, vain-talkers, and mind deceivers. They were uncontrolled because they were not allowing themselves to be placed under the authority of the church. They were vain talkers (*matailogos*). Medias means "devoid of force, truth, success, result."[29] Their speech was in vain, resultless. They were empty talkers, who uttered empty senseless things. They accomplished nothing by their futile talk. They were deceivers (*phrenapatai*),[30] meaning they were cheating, beguiling, and deceiving with fancies.

They are unruly, vain talkers and deceivers were professing (nominal) Christians, but the church needed to have them obey. The church had to silence them by putting a gag into their mouths, and thus prevent speech. "To stop the mouth" is *epistomizo*, originally meaning "to put something in the mouth."[31] This verb used metaphorically means "to reduce to silence." Some suggest that, "there were those. . . whose mouths must be stopped by the unanswerable arguments of the orthodox controversialist. This is the result hoped for from the "conviction" of verse nine."[32] They were to be answered by men who were sound in their doctrine.

These false teachers upset houses with the devastating result of having entire families in upheaval. This endangered the Christian faith. The word *anatrepo*, translated "subvert" or "discrupt," means "overturn, overthrow, and destroy."[33] The whole family would be upset the perversion of one member. They were teaching for shameful gain, "A great many religious deceivers would stop if there were no financial profit involved in their deeds."[34] The words, "teaching . . . for filthy lucre's sake" (for the sake of base gain) "refer to the claim to financial support made by itinerant or vagrant prophets and

---

[29]*Expository Dictionary* s. v. "Vain-Talkers,"

[30]*Expository Dictionary* s. v. "Mind-Decievers,"

[31]Aundt and Gingrich, *Lexicon*, 301.

[32]White, *1 and 2 Timothy and Titus*, 188.

[33]Arnt and Gingrich, *Lexicon*, 62.

[34]Kent, *The Pastoral Epistles*, 23-224.

apostles.[35] They were lying. Cretans were well known for lying.[36] The immorality of Crete was well known too.[37] Paul quotes the poet Epimerizes, himself a Cretan. A common proverb was "Cretize against" meaning, "lie to a lie."[38] The Cretan habit of lying passed into a verb *kretizi*, "to speak like a Cretan, to lie," and "into a *kretismos*, Cretan behavior, lying."[39] The reading here seems to suggest that the Cretans were wild beasts (evil beasts), meaning, they were rude, cruel, and brutal. Thus Epimerizes stated that the absence of wild beats from Crete was supplied by its human inhabitants.[40] The Cretans were "idle gluttons," and the author here has in mind the belly, as it obtrudes itself on the beholder and is a burden to the possessor. They needed to curb their appetites because they were becoming a problem to themselves.

The situation in Crete was tense and serious, and urgent action needed to be taken. They needed to be sharply rebuked. This rebuke was to be sharp and severe *(apotomos)*. *Apotmos* is from *apo* (off, from) and *temno* (cut as with a knife). They were to be sharply rebuked *(elegcho),* so as to bring conviction and confession of sin. The purpose was that of restoring to sound doctrine, "the intention of the reproof was not merely the securing of a controversial triumph, but to bring into the way of truth all such as have erred, and are deceived."[41]

They had to be warned against following Jewish myths and commandments of men (the law of a Moses with fanciful additions). They had to be warned that false teaching was an evidence of a polluted mind and conscience (henceforth their decisions and attitudes were no longer reliable guides). They had to be warned that a

---

[35]Ibid.
[36]White, *1 and 2 Timothy and Titus*, 189.
[37]Blaiklock, *The Pastoral Epistles*, 75.
[38]Wuest, *Word Studies*, 2:187.
[39]Ibid.
[40]Kent, *The Pastoral Epistles*, 224.
[41]White, *1 and 2 Timothy and Titus*, 187.

profession of knowing God may be challenged by a conduct which denies Him. Deeds must not contradict lips. All things are pure to those who are pure in heart.

Summary of Titus 1:1-16

A Christian leader must be both a servant of God and of the people he is serving. He must carry out the work that God has called him to do. He must serve diligently and faithfully as Paul did. A leader must serve the interests and causes of the people that God has called him to serve. The motivation for faithful and diligent service for the Christian leader is the "hope of everlasting life."

A Christian leader must appoint other godly men to assist him in leading the church, but such men should be men of approved Christian reputation. Strict qualifications are needed for the different categories of church officials because they are stewards of the church of God.

A Christian leader must exercise discipline in the church. Any discipline must be exercised with the aim of restoring.

The work of Christian leader is seen here to include," putting things in order the things that are lacking," meaning that a church leader should not sit and see disorderliness in the church but he/she should seek opportunity or organize the church of Christ (V. 5).

The apostle Paul is writing to Titus as "genuine child". This relationship illustrates Paul's concern for Titus (v. 4). Titus, now a shepherd or Christian leaders, needed someone to shepherd him. This is a challenge to senior Christian leaders; they should take the initiative to shepherd the more junior Christian leaders. Today, many church leaders suffer from "loneliness," they need to be cared for by someone, this calls for shepherding of shepherds.

The clause, "For this cause I left you behind in Crete," shows us that Paul, under the guidance of the Holy Spirit, made the decision to leave Titus behind. Paul, as an apostle, was owed an accountability by Titus by virtue of seniority and responsibility. There is need for one to be accountable to someone. Paul was accountable to God, but Titus was accountable to Paul. We also learn delegation of responsibility here, Paul delegated the responsibility of "putting in order," things lacking in the church in Crete.

The qualifications for church leaders in vv. 6-9 can be categorized as:

- One, the leader must be one who cannot be successfully accused. This does not mean he cannot be accused, but, when accused, he must not be found guilty.
- Two, the church is the property of God. The church leader is a steward of God's property (v. 7).
- Three, the family qualifications are to be checked before the appointment of a church leader. He must be a husband of one wife who has believing children (v. 6).
- Four, seven personality qualifications are listed (vv. 7b, 8a). These qualifications concern his daily lifestyle as a Christian. He should be not be self-pleasing, self-willed, or arrogant. He should not be easily provoked to anger or prone to anger. He should not be beside wine nor should he be a striker. He should not be greedy of gain but he should be hospitable and a lover of good.
- Five, verse 8b gives a mental qualification: he should be sound-minded (sensible).
- Finally, verse 8c and 9 give spiritual and moral qualifications of Christian leader. He must be one whose conduct meets the approval of God (righteous). The leader must be one whose conduct is true to his moral and religious obligation. He must be self-controlled and restrained not to over do anything. He must hold firm to the word of God.

These categories show us that Christian leadership involves the whole personality of the leader; his entire life is incorporated in his leadership role.

Modeling for Servant Leadership

CHAPTER THIRTEEN

Summary of the Pauline Concept of Leadership

Leadership flows out of one's commitment to the Lordship of Jesus Christ (Eph. 4:1). One must be a child of God before becoming a servant of God. Leadership begins and ends in Christ (Eph. 4:15). Christ is the Head of the church, and the model of leadership. Paul emphasizes on the centrality of Christology in leadership. In Eph.4:1, he starts with the conjunctions, "therefore " meaning that what he will continue to say depends on what he has already said. In chapters one and three Paul had been dealing with Christology. Leadership will only be effective in the church when it is Christian leadership, that is, centered in Christ. Leadership must aim at glorifying Christ, the Head of the church. A leader must be a Christian before becoming a Christian leader. Personal commitment to the Lordship of Jesus Christ is the beginning of any effective church leadership. Not until Christ is in the control of all leaders can his leadership be effective. When a committed Christian is leading, he or she is leader in place of Christ, who is the leader of His church (Eph. 1:22-23), and the Church of Christ is a living organism:

A living organism can have only one head, and the function of the head can never be delegated to other parts of the body. An institution, having no organic relationship between its individual members and its head, must delegate authority and responsibility . . .in an organism each individual part is in intimate connection with the head, and the head sends impulses and commands directly to it.

In conclusion about this first principle of Pauline concept of leader, we see leadership not as a position but as a relationship with Christ Himself (Eph 4:16). It is a Christ who is the source and origin of Christian leadership, and who supplies is to the churches leadership needs.

The second concept is that "leadership is servanthood" (Eph. 4:11). It is Christ who gave the leaders mentioned in this verse. So the leader must serve the interests of Christ. Who gave him to the Church. The leader must be a servant of Christ and a servant of the people he or she is leading.

The emphasis of Ephesians 4:1-6 is unity within the body of Christ. Leaders are a gift to the church of Christ, given by Christ Himself, so leadership must be performed within the context of unity.

The third concept is that "leadership must be body leadership" (Eph. 4:11-13). Lawrence Richards and Clyde Hoeldtke write:

> Leaders have a special function in the body. Leaders have to prepare other members for ministry. Leaders who function in this way will find the local body growing up until it reaches Unity in the faith.[1]

This leads us to believe that the functioning of leadership is to facilitate the functioning of the body under the headship of Christ (Eph. 4:11-13). Leadership facilitates growth, maturity, and increase (Eph. 4:13).

Leadership is a calling (Eph. 4:1). It is an appointment by God. It is God who entrusts a leader to an office. A leader, called to an office, must exercise humility, gentleness, patience, and forbearance (Eph. 4:3). These are great marks of any one called to the office of leadership.

Leadership calls for diligence to maintain unity in the body of Christ (Eph. 4:2-6). A leader must "take pains" to maintain that

---

[1] Richards and Holdtke, *A Theology*, 17.

unity. The whole person of a Christian leader must be involved in maintaining that unity, that is, his will, sentiment, reason, strength, and attitude. A leader only maintains a unity which already exists in believers. Believers are already in one body, the church, have one spirit, called into one hope, have one Lord and one faith, and are baptized through one baptism. If believers do not know this, the leader must teach to be sure to maintain this unity. Unity is essential for any church leadership to be effective. Unity is essential for both leaders and members to be a blessing to one another.

Unity does not mean uniformity. All believers are called to a privilege and responsibility, and so are the leaders. Both the laity and the leaders are given gifts (4:7). There is diversity in these God-given gifts. This diversity shows that each believer is important and has a responsibility. Both the ordained church leaders and the laity need one another in ministry of perfecting the saints. The Pauline concept on the functions of church the leaders listed in Eph. 4:11 is recorded in Eph. 4:12 as the preparing or equipping of saints. The word "prepare" *(katartizo)* means, "put in order, restore that is restore to its former condition and put into proper condition, complete, make complete or, as used here in Eph. 4:12, to mean to equip saints for service through training and discipline.[2] This means that church leaders are charged with the responsibility of putting the members of the body into proper condition with the aim of preparing them for works of service.

God has called some to the ministry, and has designated some to be apostles, prophets, evangelists, pastors, and teachers (Eph. 4:11-12). These are called for the purpose of building the church of God, and for the perfection of the saints. Saints are called to minister, that is, to do the work of service. Church leaders must build the church of God (the body). Church leaders must discharge their functions to a condition of making saints complete (no longer being tossed).

---

[2] Arndt and Gingrich, *Lexicon*, 418-419.

The apostle Paul mentions some of the titles of Christian leader; namely, overseers, deacons, and deaconesses (1 Tim. 3:1-16). The apostle then lists their required (standard) qualifications. In 1 Tim. 3:2-16 and in Titus 1:6-9 we have come to the conclusion that leadership is not the office of the holder, but the holder himself and the life he lives to the glory of the Lord Jesus Christ. These qualifications emphasize the spiritual and moral life of these leaders. The general qualification is that an overseer must be one who cannot be laid upon or be accused of anything. He must be morally upright, that is, a one-wife sort of husband. He must be mentally sound as seen in his personal conduct and personal habits. He must be calm and temperate. He must be sensible (serious), and must not be offensive to others. He must be dignified and orderly. He must be able to instruct. Some of the personality qualifications include a fondness of offering hospitality, not be sitting long as his wine which results in him being quarrelsome (two views are expressed, either total abstinence or over-indulgence), not being quick-tempered or quarrelsome, contentious, glorying in argument, and not being fond of money. Paul then lists the domestic qualifications which are the ability to preside over his household and control over his children so that they live in obedience and subjection. The overseer must not be a novice, that is, a new convert, because his elevation can build conceit and confusion to him and to the church. He must be of good reputation to those outside the church. The term "overseer" refers to bishops and pastors.

In 1 Tim. 3:8-13, Paul lists the qualifications for deacons. These church leaders were charged with the ministry of the temporal welfare of the church. The standard requirements listed here also apply to all the areas of their lives. They must be dignified people, worthy of respect because of their seriousness of mind and their character. They must not be double-tongued, saying one thing and meaning another, or giving representations to different people about the same thing. They should not attach themselves to wine. Our view is that of 'no wine at all' although the context allows the view of 'no abusive use of wine,' They should not be lovers of disgraceful gain, that is, they should be honest, and not embezzle funds. The office of a deacon cannot be separated from the deacons' life. A deacon must be known to be practicing his Christian faith, because Christian faith and daily living are intimately tied together.

The apostle then writes, "these also," meaning that the deacon and the overseers already discussed must be proved before appointment. Christian experience of candidates must be considered before appointment. They must be people who have undergone a constant observing, and thus proved to be inaccessible (beyond reproach).

The next verse 1 Tim. 3:11 concerning the 'wives' refers to deaconesses. They must be dignified and serious with their work. They must not be slanderers because they do not belong to the devil, the slanderer. They must faithful in all things, that is, faithful to their ministry, to Christ, and to their husbands.

The apostle Paul once again refers to the deacons, already referred to in 1 Tim. 3:8-10. The domestic qualification is not left out because success or failure of a person intended to hold the office of a deacon can be seen at home. As with the bishop, he must be a 'one wife sort of a husband.' He must be a good manager under habitual instruction written here in 1 Tim. 3:15 shows that all these qualifications should be followed, without exemptions, for all who work in the household of God, the church. Titus 1:1 deals with the person of the apostle Paul. Paul was an apostle and a servant of God. A leader must view himself as a servant of God. Paul served God with the motivation of "hope for eternal life," A church leader though serving his fellow men must know that he is serving God. A leader's motivation for ministry must be the hope of everlasting life.

The apostle in verse 5 instructed Titus to appoint elders. We have already noted that elders and overseers were the same people. Titus needed the elders. To appoint them meant that he would not do all ministries by himself alone. The ministry in the church is not a one-man game, or a one man show. Ministry is partnership among the saints. Ministry is completing one another by our God-given gifts.

The apostle lists in Titus 1:6 the qualifications for elders (also called overseers in verse 7). They must be above reproach, men of unquestionable integrity. They must be men who cannot be called into question, men who have lived an exemplary life of holiness that no accusation can be brought against them. They must have the family qualifications listed in Titus 1:6 and in 1 Tim. 3:2-13 both deacons and overseers. They must be the husband of one wife, morally pure, and with no relationship outside their marriages. They must not be people who are self-willed or self-pleasing nor should they be people who cannot control their anger. They should not be people who are always beside their wine nor should they be men of greedy gain. They must be lovers of what is good, both good men and good things. Their spiritual and moral qualifications are righteousness, holiness. Self-control, faithfulness in holding to the word, and the ability to exhort in right doctrine and to refute those who contradict it.

The apostle also states that rebellious men, empty talkers, and deceivers must be disciplined. The severe discipline must aim not at destroying but at restoring. Church leaders must discipline with the aim of restoring. These qualifications must be adhered to according to these instructions, and Titus was asked to use them in his selection of elders.

In our study of the Pauline concept of leadership in Ephesians 4:1-16, 1 Tim. 3:1-16, and Titus 1:1-16, the leadership tilter or leaders placed in church are: Apostles, prophets, Evangelists, pastor, Teachers, Overseers, Elders, Deacons, and Deaconess. We notice that in most cases, these terms are used interchangeable despite of the fact that functionally there are some distinctions. When we can see Paul making a distinction in scope of leadership, it is either in a local role or in a whole church role. This should not be seen to mean that church leadership should be institutionalized nor should the church leader be seen as a manager or a decision maker. The church leader is called to care and nurture the believers (Eph. 4:12).

Part Three: Church Leadership: The Kenyan Experience

CHAPTER FOURTEEN

Church Leadership in Kenya: An Overview

Introduction

The church in Kenya has had a phenomenal growth. One author, writing on Kenyan churches, stated: "In Kenya five hundred thousand people in a year are joining the Christian faith, and there are five million practicing Christians."[1] In 1962, fifty-three percent of the Kenyan population was Christian, and by 1972, the figure had risen to sixty-six percent. By the year two thousand, it is estimated that the population will be 40 Million, and that eighty-three percent of the population will be Christians.[2] This serves as evidence to show that the Christian faith is growing at a meteoric rate. While Kenya has two hundred and nine-two denominations that are registered under the Societies' Act of the Kenya government, many independent churches are mushrooming day after day to the point where the government is no longer registering them. In an article entitled, "No more new churches, "the following was reported:

---

[1] David B. Barrett, "The Expansion of Christianity in Kenya AD 1900-2000," in *Kenya Churches Handbook* (Evangel Publishing House, 1973), 157.

[2] Ibid., 160.

Among the controversial decisions that the Kenya's attorney-general, Mr. Justice Mathew Muli has taken recently is to stop registering any new churches or splinter churches in the country. Muli told a voice of Kenya television press conference a fortnight ago that the government would not register any more splinter churches, and that those already registered will be investigated with a view of deregistering some of them.[3]

Kenya is well known all over Africa, if not all over the world, for her Christian growth as well as her denominational growth. Political stability has contributed towards evangelization, and, with peace, love, and unity, people carrying the God News are able to move freely to proclaim the gospel.

However, one recent report said,

> The Vatican is worried about the mushrooming of bogus sects in some countries, among them Kenya, which has the highest number of registered churches in the world. The All Africa Press services reports that the country has over eight hundred religious groups but less that fourteen are genuine. Many have broken away from major churches, and operate on commercial basis taking advantage of the prevailing "spiritual vacuum."[4]

The mushrooming of independent churches has been attributed to several factors that involve the church leaders. Some independent churches have been formed because of church discipline in the established church. When some Christians are disciplined by the leaders, they gather those who sympathize with them or others in similar circumstances to form an independent group. Another factor is the failure of one party to be sympathetic to another party's point of view. A third factor is the desire of strong personality to be indepen-

---

[3] Hilary Ngw'eno "No more New Churches," *Weekly Review*, 9 November 1984, 13-15.

[4] "Vatican Alarmed over Rebel Churches," *Nation* 23 May 1986, 3.

dent and direct his own group according to his own interests. A fourth factor is the restriction of one's activities by a church council.[5] Finally, some schisms or splits are over the question of policy or leadership.[6] Poor leadership, lack of Christian love, understanding and sympathy all can cause disastrous leadership problems.

In 1973, the population of Kenya was around twelve million, of which eight and one-half million were professing Christians. This was 68.3 percent of the total population. The Christian increase is now 2.1 percent each year.[7] The African continent as a whole is said to have a phenomenon growth of four thousand converts every day.[8] It is estimated that by the year two thousand, the Christian population will be twenty eight and one half million people.[9] The official government statement on population said:

> When the 1962 population census was conducted, the results revealed a total count of just 8.6 million people. By 1969, it had risen to 10.9 million and it reached 15.3 million by 1979. The high growth of Kenya's population is a consequence of increasing fertility and declining mortality. It is projected that if fertility and mortality remain unchanged, the population of Kenya will be 24.9 million by 1990 and thirty five million by the year 2000.[10]

---

[5] Peter Falk, *The Growth of the Church in Africa*, (Grand Rapids, Michigan: Zondervan Publishing House, 1976), 457.

[6] Barret, "*Varieties of Kikuyu Independent Churches*," in Kenya Churches Handbook, 129-130.

[7] Barrett, "*The Expansion*," 160.

[8] The Association of Evangelicals of Africa and Madagascar, "Proceedings of A.E.A.M. 4th Assembly Malawi," *Church in Africa Today and Tomorrow*, (Nairobi, Kenya: Evangel Publishing House, 1984), v i i.

[9] Barrett, "The Expansion," 170.

[10] Republic of Kenya, Ministry of Finance and Planning. *Central Bureau of Statistics*. Economic Survey 1984, May 1984, 30.

In this population there are three categories of Christians to be found:

> First, professing Christians, those whose religious preference is Christianity and profess, 'I am a Christian, 'particularly in a government census or a public opinion poll. Secondly, affliated Christians these are Christians affiliated to churches which means all those known to be the churches. On the church's' rolls, books or records, and therefore claimed by the church in their statistics. Third, practicing Christians, active Christians, or participation Christians, which means those who attend church activities regularly.[11]

The Christian faith will continue to grow in Kenya for the following reasons. First, the political stability allows many Christians who are committed to evangelism to go out freely and share the gospel.

The Constitution of Kenya provides that except with his own consent, no person shall be hindered in the enjoyment of his freedom of conscience, and for the purposes of this section the said freedom includes freedom of thought and of religion, freedom to change his religion or belief, and freedom, either alone or in community with others, and both in public and in private, to manifest and propagate his religion or belief in worship, teaching, practice, and observance.[12]

Second, there is a growing co-operation and understanding among Christians.[13] The old antagonistic attitude among Christians is dying.[14] Before political independence in Kenya on the 12th of December 1964, Christian denominations were antagonistic towards one another. Kenya was then divided into districts to avoid duplication of ministry as well as to lessen the antagonism.

Different denominations were given different districts which they would concentrate on as they introduced Christianity to Africans. Nationalism always distorts the vision of Christians with a

---

[11]Ibid., 165-166.
[12]Kenya, *Constitution*, 41.
[13]Barrett, "The Expansion," 177.
[14]Abid., 168-169.

national self-righteousness, and as a result some are seen as nationalists, others as collaborators (hypocrites). "The hypocrites, Judases, and *thaka* (stooges, traitors) included chiefs, government servants and anyone hostile to the (Mau Mau) movement, many of whom were Christians from mission churches."[15] When it came to outing, hostility and violence were experienced by Christians, especially the Revivalist Christians who objected to it.[16]

Africanization of church leadership was there in principle but the goal of giving supreme responsibility to African Christians by the missionaries was either postponed or neglected.[17] Faced with Uhuru or a church revolt, missions hastily handed over authority. This Africanization in one way or the other brought with it attitudes of rivalry among Christians, leaders, and their foreign Christian masters. Today the story is different:

> If one turns to any of the modern states-Ghana, Nigeria, Zaire, Rhodesia, Kenya, Uganda—and investigates the early decades of this century, one is faced with an incredible story of Christian vitality, creativity, and commitment. There was usually intense rivalry, which can now be called in more mellow and irenic times.[18]

Today there is a harmonious relationship in spite of the fact that, at first, protestant missions in Kenya and Tanzania practiced comity, for they considered that the essential ministry was preaching the Gospel and that preaching should not be sabotaged by wasteful competition.[19] The antagonistic attitude towards one another is seen as being against the word of God (Eph. 4), and cooperation has permit-

---

[15] William B. Anderson, *The Church in East Africa 1840-1974*, (Nairobi, Kenya: Uzima Press, 1977), 129.

[16] Ibid., 130.

[17] Ibid., 143.

[18] Elliott Kendall, *The End of an Era*, (London: The Society of promoting Christian knowledge, 1978), 67.

[19] Anderson, *The Church,* 130.

ted church bodies to undertake significant responsibility that one body could not undertake alone, such as training colleges (St. Paul's United Theological college, Pan Africa Christian College) and appointing of education counselors (chaplains in Kenya universities and secondary schools).[20] The younger people are not hostile to Christianity but to cultural arrogance of the anthropologists.[21]

Third, there is growth of training facilities for the afro-ministers. Local Christians are being trained for local ministry. The church in Kenya is encouraging the building of an indigenous church which is self-ruling, self-propagation, and self-supporting. To have a highly-trained, highly-skilled, and experienced leadership, the church in Kenya opened many institutions of advanced learning such as Bible schools, colleges, seminaries, and universities.[22]

Fourth, youth are a critical section of the Kenyan society (covering sixty percent of total population).[23] The church in Kenya faced with a big challenge because of having a large portion of younger people forming a big fraction of the Kenya population. The government states that, the number of the younger population is growing first. Education being one of the most important influences on the quality of life, then resources must be geared toward education. The government must also must provided better educational systems to provide the basis for the technology to sustain and improve the quality of life... education in Kenya has expanded rapidly since Independence from 0.9 million in 1963 to the number of educated people in 1983.[24] With the current birth rate, the number of young people will increase and, if well ministered to, the church will grow. Young people who are well trained are taking up leadership and are using their ministry skills to teach people.

---

[20]Falk, *The Growth*, 465.
[21]Kendall, *The End*, 94
[22]Anderson, *The Church*, 163.
[23]Falk, *The Growth*, 467-468.
[24]Economic Survey 84, 35-36.

Fifth, more and more people are becoming literate. The current literacy rate for Kenya is forty-five percent.[25] With the present increased rate of literacy, many can read the good news for themselves and come to a decision of following Christ. The church press is utilized for this purpose.[26]

Sixth, Christianity has previously been seen as a "white man's religion" connected with colonialism. The older people with this attitude are now being outgrown by a younger generation which is more responsive and positive towards Christianity:

> The Christian faith today is not the novelty it was fifty years ago, an invention for a few which could be tried and then thrown away if not useful. It is now being authenticated by people in practically every ethic group in the Republic.[27]

This shows a good growth in understanding what is becoming a Christian means.

Seventh, many lay people are sharing the gospel while others lead people to Christ through their exemplary living.[28] Eighth, mass media has been a very useful way of reaching people with the Gospel.[29]

Church Leadership and Politics

Independence from British colonialism, commonly known as *Uhuru,* was very stimulating to the churches in Kenya, "Uhuru in East Africa was an event itself with great religious overtones . . . during

---

[25] Enver Carim, ed., *Africa Guide 84*, s. v. "Kenya," (Essex, England: World Information, 1984), 173.

[26] Anderson, *The Church*, 165.

[27] Barret, *Kenya's cultural Heritage and Tradition,* in Kenya Churches Handbook, 40-42.

[28] Falk, *The Growth*, 430.

[29] Barret, *"Religious Broadcasting in Kenya,"* in Kenya Churches Handbook, 85-94.

the Uhuru period, Kenyan and Kenya Christianity came to the forefront."[30] On Kenya becoming an independent state, there was a cordial relationship between the church and the state, despite the antagonistic towards Christianity seen in the pre-uhuru days, when nationalists (Mau-Mau fighters) produced political hymns which were sung at the rallies . . . and used Christian hymn tunes . . . when outing broke out, hostility was directed against Christianity.[31]

On the 12th of December 1964, Kenya's Independence Day, church leaders prayed before the swearing in of the president, Mzee Jomo Kenyatta. On all major national days Church leaders pray in almost every government function, all of which tend to begin with prayer. A cordial relationship has existed between the church and politicians. Political freedom and the freedom of religious expression has promoted a working relationship and partnership between the church and politicians. Freedom of expression is enshrined in the Kenya constitution, Section V of which contains Kenya's version of the Bill of Rights. A problem only come when church leaders and the citizens join hands to face an evil in the government. The church leaders, on doing this, have been asked to stick to their preaching ministry, and not to be involved in the so-called "dirty game" of politics. For example, in 1983, a local magazine reported, "the minister of Energy and Regional Development, Mr. Nicholas Biwott, 'advised church leaders who want to join politics to first quit their positions as church leaders.'"[32]

In an article entitled, "Christians and the State," the following was stated:

> Archbishop Kuria of the church of the province of Kenya . . . found himself in trouble when he seemed to question the extent to which Kenyans had attained spiritual and moral freedom in addition

---

[30] Anderson, *The Church*, 128.
[31] Ibid., 129.
[32] J. Martin Weke, "Church Going Statesman," sign-post, Vol. 1 number 4, 11.

to political freedom . . . Christians had a dual loyalty, firstly to God, and secondly to the state . . . the central issue is the nature of free speech in Kenya today . . Governments sometimes may not appreciate that the Christian occasions when he (the Christian leader) is critical and revelatory.[33]

One politician, speaking to church leaders, was quoted as saying that church leaders and the laity should not be afraid to speak out if society has gone wrong. Local church leaders and the laity must be the conscience of society in which they live.[34] Church leaders have had a strong and cordial relationship with the Kenya head of state to the point of being entertained in his official residence where he once addressed them was reported as telling them that "religion was not a privilege but a right and that churches should regard themselves as part and parcel of the government.[35] This relationship is also seen in the statement of the Kenyan vice-president who was quoted as saying, "politics and religion are inseparable. To suggest that politics should be left to the politicians and religion to the clergy is terrible intellectual arrogance."[36]

On the other hand, there are those politicians who hold that church leaders must only preach and leave politics to politicians. For example, retired President Daniel Arap Moi "told church leaders in Kenya to serve only one master and those interested in politics to join politics and leave the church leadership."[37] On the question of church leaders' involvement with politics, some church leaders have been quoted saying:

---

[33] Robert Anderson, "Christians and the State," *Weekly Review*, 3 August 1984, 21.

[34] Henry Okullu, *Quest for Justice: A Biblical Mandate*, (Nairobi, Kenya: Uzima press, 1984). 3.

[35] Ibid., 53.

[36] Ibid.

[37] Weke, *Church Going*, 10.

> The church will never 'abdicate' its role in shaping the political destiny of Kenya... the church does not just have a right to participate in political affairs, but a 'duty'... political matters were as much a concern to clerics as they were to every other citizen. Politicians must leave the church alone. Kuria has gone as far as to denounce the 'Leave politics to politicians' call as an empty cliché.[38]

The contention between church leaders and politicians in Kenya is first of all on involvement in each other's field. Secondly, there are those who see freedom of expression enshrined in the Kenya government constitution as a government-given freedom, and those who see this freedom as God-given and the government is obligated to protect it. The constitution states,

> Except with his own consent, no person shall be hindered by the enjoyment of his freedom of expression, that is to say, freedom to hold opinions without interference, freedom to receive ideas and information without interference.[39]

Many Kenya church leaders feel that public statements and private opinions should be the same. Politicians, however, speak at times as individuals, while at other times they speak in a quite different fashion as national leaders:

> Kenyatta (founder of the Kenyan nation) refused to attach himself to any organized religion, but he believed in God (as the Kikuyu do), and all his political speeches were full of biblical references. He maintained in his public addresses that no religion or church, in the case of Christian come with a western covering)... president Moi is a church goer, and a member of the Africa Inland Church... often addresses the congregations during or after worship... is open to advice...[40]

---

[38] Ng'weno, "PCEA Row as Wanjau Is Installed," *Weekly Review*, 3 May 1985, 10

[39] Kenya, *Constitution*, 42.

[40] Weke, "*Church Going,*" 10.

The role of the church is not well understood by some of our political leaders. Some see the church as the "praying department" of the government. One politician was quoted as saying, "the country guaranteed freedom of worship and prayers for peace."[41] The church leaders felt obligated to pray for the peace of the nation in spite of the fact that one politician was quoted saying, "people should not ask God for peace which he had already given."[42]

The election of church leaders has been an issue of discussion for some time now. Politicians have been an issue of discussion for some time now. Politicians have been accused of involvement in the selection and election of church leaders. The rule of the thumb is that, "State officials cannot and should not exert pressure on the appointment of church leaders, and politicians cannot intrude on the inner life of the church."[43] We believe that there is a misunderstanding in this area. A politician who is a member of certain denomination had every right to participate in the elections of the church leaders. The problem comes when a politician influences the elections by virtue of this office.

Church Leadership and Finances

The missionaries who came to Kenya since 1900 did not ask for financial support from the Kenyan Christians. Today the result has been that "for many catholic and protestant members, mission and giving mean contribution to those representative workers who are at work overseas."[44] The Christians therefore never felt obligated to support the church, and if they did so, they were reluctant in their giving. With the coming of Uhuru, and the advocating of Africanization, two things happened to the church.

---

[41] Ibid., 11.
[42] Kendall, *The End*, 117.
[43] Okullu, "Church State Relationship," 64.
[44] Anderson, *The Church*, 145.

First, the missionaries left hastily or unwillingly.[45] Today there are many more missionaries in Para-church organizations but not in the main line denomination. This meant, in most of the cases, the withdrawal of financial support.[46] Many that supported churches maintained a paternalistic and superior attitude.[47]

Second, with the coming of Uhuru, also came *Harambee* (pulling together) which was an expression of African socialism. On 1 June 1963, the late president of Kenya, Mzee Jomo Kenyatta said, "We must work harder to fight our enemies (namely), ignorance, sickness, and poverty. I therefore give you the call: *HARAMBEE!* Left us all work hard together for our country, Kenya."[48] These intentions, which originally were very noble, have been over played because the original objective of raising money for particular projects was gradually turned to be a way to hold political rallies. This change of emphasis has now become a thorn in the flesh for the church:

> The dilemma now facing the churches is whether or not to continue with the practice of inviting politicians to preside over their harambee fund raising meetings, and thus provide the guest with a church platform for political activities and electioneering.[49]

Clergy and Laity in Church Leadership

The gaining of political independence (*uhuru*) resulted in Africanization, and local Christians had now to take up the responsibility of church leadership. Even today, full Africanization is still either neglected, overlooked, or postponed in some of the denominations,

---

[45] Kendall, *The End*, 94-95.
[46] Ibid., 101.
[47] Jomo Kenyatta, *Harambee*, (Nairobi, Kenya: Oxford University Press, 1964), 7.
[48] Okullu, "Church State Relationship," 56.
[49] Kendall, *The End*, 57-58.

The development of leadership and personalities among the missionary community, stipulated by the special circumstances of the mission and the cultural advantage, made it much more difficult for Africans to achieve positions of equal leadership. Potential African leaders could not easily push through the suffocation layer of senior missionaries. Relics of this situation remain, so that it can be examined and experienced at first-hand today.[50]

One author noted, "There was abundant evidence to show that the seeming popularity of missionary leadership only masked a deep unease about its reliability and a resentment of its assertion."[51] Previously Africanization was accomplished in the essential work of evangelization and pastoral care, but not in leadership positions. An author noted:

> Faced with Uhuru, or a church revolt, missions hastily handed over authority ... the importance of Africanization cannot be underestimated independent sprang up in some cases because African Christians believed African leadership was necessary for a genuinely African Christianity.[52]

The African church, which was growing at a meteoric rate, had not trained men to take up leadership. The people who were originally doing evangelistic work had now to take up leadership positions. These leaders were church members who had gifts for service and sincere devotion to the Lord. The bishop, pastors, evangelists, and catechists were chosen from among the faithful and training by their missions both locally and abroad but, "pastoral candidates were expected to manifest intellectual, social, and spiritual qualifications as

---

[50]Ibid.

[51]R. Macqherson, *The Presbyterian Church in Kenya*, (Kenya Litho Ltd., 1970), 145.

[52]Anderson, *The Church*, 145.

judged by Western standards in order to qualify to serve as pastors."[53]

While Western standards of qualification may be checked in candidate for church leadership, spiritual leadership gifts and sincere dedication should be standards are not important and therefore should be withdrawn. Rather, culturally relevant qualifications should be emphasized. One church leader who had spiritual leadership gifts, ability, and dedication yet without academic qualification, was the late Bishop Kariuki, whom God used mightily. At his burial, due to his exemplary church leadership, the following words were given as a testimony: "The words of Njiri Karago in his eulogy fairly sum up Obadiah Kariuki's life: As we say farewell to the warrior, let us recall the words of our lord: 'be faithful unto death and I will give thee the crown of life."[54]

We must note that the problems of Africanization of church leadership after political independence have persisted to this day. Since then, there has been either a crushed program of leadership training, hasty promotion of church leader, or appointment of wrong people to positions of leadership. The church has either taken the wrong people for training, or given wrong people the wrong position. After training, some of the younger men have not been accepted for leadership positions.[55]

The church in Kenya has enjoyed fellowship amongst the clergy and laity. A growing church has desperately needed leaders. One ordained pastor may be leading twelve to twenty congregations. This has forced the ordained men to lay people, some of whom are not well trained. In 1972, there were six thousand clergymen who were ministering to four million Christians. In the year 2000 and

---

[53]Falk, *The Growth*, 440

[54]Obadiah Kariuki, A *Bishop Facing Mount Kenya; An autobiography, 1902 – 1978*, Trans. George Mathu (Nairobi, Kenya: Uzuma Press Limited, 1985), 114.

[55]Falk, *The Growth*, 442-444.

beyond, it is estimated that there will be more than 20,000 clergymen ministering to 15 million Christians.[56]

The using of untrained people for leadership in churches has its own problems and its blessings. Whether the ordained minister is present or not, church ministries continue. Christians are ministered to by a person who knows them well. The pastor is referred to only when the lay leaders cannot cope with a particular issue or problem. Due to the scarcity of ordained ministers, lay ministry has been a blessing to the church in Africa.[57] The problems we have seen in using lay leaders comes when we do not train them well. They are well informed as to how far they can go in making a decision. They sometimes go too far in a particular issue without referring to the pastor. When the pastor hears of it, he feels unrecognized, and looked down upon. This may come because the pastor is far away and out of reach. The pastor becomes a supervisor, just going round to check what the lay people are doing. This means he is not able to minister to the needs of the people, and is not a shepherd to them. The pastor also becomes a stranger to the congregation, having no authority over the laity.

The lay leader builds power around himself and the problem comes when the pastor interferes. With the pastor's authority being undermined some pastors have been forced by lay leaders to do things that are unbiblical. On the other hand, some clergy have caused the lay leader problems. Some have been known to choose people who do not qualify by their life, or people without the spirit of submission to them as their spiritual leaders. Others use their appointed authority to force decisions that do not fit the local situation.

Church Leadership Meetings

Church leadership meetings are called for the purpose of discussing issues that relate to the building of the entire body of Christ. Differ-

---

[56]Barrett, "The Expansion," 160.
[57]Falk, *The Growth*, 442.

ent denominations in Kenya use different names for these meetings. For example, the church of the province of Kenya (Anglican) has the council, parish council, Diocesan synod, and the Provincial Synod. All these councils are comprised of people who are elected by the congregations to be action as their representatives. Another example is the Presbyterian Church of East Africa. They have an Elders Council, a Kirk session Council, Presbytery Council, and the General Assembly. All these councils are comprised of lay church elders as well as the clergy.

These church leadership councils discuss spiritual, financial, and administrative matters of the church. Kenya, with more than two hundred known denominations, has but perhaps a few of them being led run by single individuals. Church leadership is done by councils, or decisions for the leader are decided by committees or councils. One church described parish council:

> The function of a parish council shall be: To co-operate with the parish priest in the initiation, conduct and development of church work within the parish with a view to establishing the truth of the Gospel more widely and deeply in the hearts of the people and preparing them for effective witness within the parish, to prepare an annual Budget in respect of the ensuing financial year for presentation to the Annual parish meeting, to appoint if it so desires a Finance committee and to elect from among its members the chairman of such committee, to arrange for the audition of church Accounts (auditors having been appointed by the Annual parish meeting); to submit the audited accounts to the Annual parish meeting and to the Diocesan Treasure, to co-operate with the Board on pastoral work in the selection of the parish priest, to consult with the parish priest on the appointment of curates as may be required, to established such local committee as shall be found necessary and determine their constitution and functions due regard being had both to local interests and to the well being of the parish as a whole, to appoint from among its members the Vice-Chairman of the Council and to draw up rules of

procedure provided that these are not at variance with the general principles on procedure set forth in these Regulations.[58]

Some of the meetings for the church leaders have done wonderful jobs in the running of churches in Kenya. They have been able to organize crusades, house evangelism, camps, and Bible study groups. They have used them for the propagating of the Gospel of Jesus Christ. Some have been able to build up magnificent church buildings.

On the other hand, some of the meetings have been a poor testimony both to the people they lead and those outside the church. Some have been fighting grounds. Of one Presbyterian meeting, for example, it was reported that:

> Issues raised at the meeting indicated that the church has in recent times been undergoing one of its most serious leadership crises since its independence from the Church of Scotland twenty-nine years ago. Bones of contention ranged from the struggle for church leadership to the relationship between church and state, church investment policies, tribalism and nepotism.[59]

Another example can be seen from a report on a statement issued by a college of electors, saying, "that the election was being used to expose the rift that is in their house ... the statement claimed that there was a major division in the House of Bishops and the majority of bishops had boycotted a holy communion service."[60] Some leadership meetings have been so difficult that the government administration has been forced to step in. For example, one bishop was being taken to court by other bishops. It was reported "At the end of

---

[58]Church of the Province of Kenya, Constitution as Revised at 29th November, 1979, (Nairobi, Kenya: Uzima Press Limited, 1979), 92.

[59]Ng'weno, "PCEA Row," 4.

[60]Ng'weno "Exposing the Rift", *Weekly Review*, 29 June 1984, 10.

the day, both parties told newsmen that the controversy had been resolved "amicable" before plat in the chambers."⁶¹

Another example is seen in the government being called in to supervise a church election as happened in the following media report:

> (the church) has for a long time been bedeviled with squabbles to the extent that the Provincial Administration and even the police have had to intervene to maintain harmony. The government ordered elections for leaders in the church to be held under the supervision of the District commissioner."⁶²

As a final example, some church leaders held an illegal parish council in which they made a resolution and dismissed pastor. The pastor maintained:

> . . . this parish council cannot be binding at all as this was an unconstitutional meeting convened against the standing rules and regulations governing such matters. Moreover, the ten members did not constitute the required one-third quorum."⁶³

These are just a few that are brought out to the press and to the attention of the Kenyan Christians, but it is our belief that there are many other controversial meetings that do not receive press coverage.

Accusations Leveled Against church Leaders

Any growing church, in Kenya church, has problems and challenges that come with growth. Leaders, however effective in their leadership, have burned out. The lives of others are not "beyond reproach." Church leaders have received accusations from within and without

---

⁶¹Ng'weno, "Scathing attack," *Weekly Review*, 22 June 1984, 12.
⁶²Ibid.
⁶³Ngw'eno, "More Wrangles,"*Weekly Review*, 3 August 1984, 10.

the church. One author, writing on the church in Africa (with Kenya included), stated,

> The church in Africa is far from being perfect. Among the main weaknesses are divisions and disunity within the church. This is partly a result of the fact that Christianity came to Africa in fragments represented by the biblical message of the unity and brotherhood of believers. In addition to that, there are thousands of splinter groups. Majority of them for no sound Biblical reason.[64]

Division and disunity can be seen within a local congregation, within leadership in a group of churches, or within leaders of a particular denomination nation-wide. Some causes include:

> firstly, a person may experience a struggle with himself . . . secondly, differences between people which are not related to primary issues (personality conflicts) . . . thirdly, personal values (two values, African and Western) . . . fourthly, priorities and goals . . .fifthly, cultural patterns."[65]

Church leaders have been accused of jealousies and competition. They are also said to be introducing cultural patterns of worship in churches with the aim of making an African blend of church, commonly referred to as made in Africa. Cheating in elections of church officials (leaders) has become a major accusation to church leaders. One leader was accused in a court of law for trying to impose a particular candidate upon the people in order to protect his position and interests.[66] A group of church leaders was accused of traveling long distances to campaign for a particular candidate from their tribe,

---

[64] Association of Evangelicals, *Church in Africa*, vii.

[65] Bedan Mbugua, "Church fights: Causes and Cures," *Beyond*, June 1985, 4.

[66] Ng'weno, "Scathing Atttack," 12.

and thereby encouraged tribalism, nepotism, and sectionalism.[67] Some leaders have been accused of not following biblical principles in solving church related problems such as discipline and disagreements. Other church leaders have been accused of corruption in general:

> In the church we sit down, to wait for the pastor and the elders. And when they come in, we all stand up in respect. As their lives are most corrupt, they serve the Lord in hypocrisy, a thing so lamentable.[68]

In our research we come across many articles which accused church leaders of nepotism, racialism, and sectionalism. A Christian leader said, "tribalism, sectionalism, and nepotism were found in nearly every Christian church in the country."[69] These accusations are leveled towards the African church leaders as well as the missionaries in Kenya.[70]

The church in Kenya is pulling up her own socks in meeting her financial needs. An author wrote,

> Africa as a whole is a continent of poverty. Eighty percent of the national wealth is enjoyed and controlled by five percent of the population ... in brief, it is the problem of power, poverty, and class struggle.[71]

The financial struggle has become a major struggle. In our research we found several articles on this issue which can be summarized by this statement:

---

[67] Ibid., "*PCEA Row*," 4.

[68] J. M. Miano, *Hyenas In The Church*, (Nairobi, Kenya: Uzima Press Limited, 1981), 8.

[69] Ng;weno "*PCEA Row*," 4.

[70] Anderson, *The Church*, 174.

[71] Association of Evangelicals, *Church in Africa*, viii.

there are money scandals and misuse of funds through lack of experience as much as through dishonesty. The pipes which carry foreign aid, and the tanks which store parish funds, leak. In one area an observer stated that some pastors would have to work one hundred and thirty-five years to repay the loans they have received.[72]

Some of the church leaders have been accused of using church property for their own personal activities while others have been accused of neglect of their office and pastoral duties.

---

[72] Anderson, *The Church*, 174-175.

Modeling for Servant Leadership

CHAPTER FIFTEEN

Church Leadership in Kenya in Light of Biblical Principles of Leadership

Africanization and Indigenization of Christian Leadership

It is our conviction that the church leaders in Kenya are far from being perfect. The church leaders may have strong point of leadership which we thank God for and would encourage them to make them even stronger. Some have formed denominational missionary associations. They should continually strengthen such associations. Others have lived Christ-centered lives which have resulted in effective church leadership.

Post-Uhuru days have been difficult times for most of the church leaders. There have been times when church leaders have had to stand firm for their Christian convictions and have said, "let leaders remain a herald voice in the wilderness." For example, in the 2005 and 2010 Constitution Referudum,the church reimed a prophetic voice, both witin the church and in the national life of Kenya.

To solve the present church leadership crisis in growing church, the African church is improving in the area of training. With more Bible schools, colleges, and seminaries on the African soil, training is done in the same cultural setting with culturally relevant programmers. For those already in the ministry, and for lay leaders, Theological Education by Extension programs have been emphasized and made available. Boards and committees have been formed as 'examining chaplains' check on the quality of life, devotion to the Lord, and spiritual leadership gifts of the would be church leaders. On the selection or election of church leaders, political leaders should not exert pressure for the appointment. The church should be left alone to elect her own leaders.

According to our study of St. Paul's model of leadership, church leaders must be checked and scrutinized before their appointment. This will involve proving them and checking their lives before appointing them. Leaders must be committed Christians who are known to be living their Christian faith. This point of "proving" must be emphasized for church leaders. The hasty or crash leadership training should be stopped, because it gives Satan a chance of accusing the church and can cause pride in the church leaders.

Unity and Diversity

The church is a unity in diversity (Eph. 4:7). The clergy and the laity must work together. Each must use the God-given gifts in the ministry of perfecting of the saints. To avoid the clashes between the clergy and the laity, proper training should be given as well as getting the right people (spiritual men-full of the spirit) for spiritual leadership. Each should be made to understand the scope of his ministry and to what point he can go alone without a recommendation of the church.

Unity is an essential part of the church of Christ (Eph. 4:2-6), and church leaders have no choice. Denominations or local congregations are called to a unity but not to uniformity. Church leaders must not major in the minors but on the majors of Christian belief.

Unity does not only refer to a nation or a denominational boundary but also to a universal unity of the church. The Christians in the developed countries must have unity with the so called third world Christians. The Western traditions or coverings which came with Christianity should not cause division in the church. They should be rejected but the church must remain one.

Our study of 1 Tim. 3:1-6 and Titus 1:1-16 has shown us the need of getting people with high qualifications for the high calling of leadership in the church of Christ. These qualifications must be taken seriously by the church in Kenya in appointment of her leaders.

An overview of the accusations leveled against church leaders portrays a problem of carnality in Christian leaders. For example, Christian leaders should not campaign for church leadership positions, they should pray and fast, and God will show them the person to be appointed. The Pauline model or leadership does not allow the exercising of tribalism, racialism, sectionalism, or nepotism.

Christian leadership is a calling (Eph. 4:1) from God. He appoints and entrusts a Christian to a leadership office. God's will must be sought first before an appointment of a church leader. We highly condemn individuals or tribal leaders who think that Christian leaders should be elected by virtue of their ethnic backgrounds when they do not biblically qualify for leadership positions. Our view is that a Christian leader may not necessarily be a tribal leader.

A Christian leader must have the four essential marks which are humility (gentleness, courtesy, considerateness), meekness (disciplined and controlled), patience (slow in avenging and striving for harmony), and love (seeking the highest good of others). Our view of the Pauline model of leadership does not agree with Christian leaders who use unpiloted or abusive language when they are provoked or when they are condemning political abuse of power or injustice in society.

Christian leaders, as the 'salt' and 'light', must be disciplined and controlled in their private and public life, and in their exerting of leadership functions. The prophetic ministry of the Christian leaders, who are the conscience of society, should be exercised conviction, discipline, and control so that it will be a blessing to those who are its recipients.

Christian leaders must always 'strive' and 'take pains' to maintain harmony and unity in the Christian society. Our view of Christian leadership sees Christian leaders who cause division and disunity in the church as contradicting their call. Peace must be maintained because peace holds and preserves unity within the church.

Unity in the church does not mean uniformity, therefore Christian leaders must realize that the saints have their God-given gifts which they will have to be allowed to use in the body, the church. Christian leaders are only a part of the divine plan of leadership, which is shared participation (Eph. 4:4-6). Christian leadership is a shared privilege and responsibility, therefore Christian leaders must delegate (Eph. 4:7-16). We find a Christian leader who makes church leadership a 'one man show' inconsistent with the Pauline model of leadership.

Leaders as a Gift to the Church

The apostles, prophets, evangelists, pastors, and teachers named in Eph. 4:11-12 are given as gifts to the church, by God, for the purpose of building the church of Christ. The leaders are to train the saints for the works of service. Christian leadership involves teaching and training as methods of equipping the saints, therefore a Christian leader is an equipper of saints. In the process of teaching and training, the Christian leader sharpens the God-given gifts to meet the specific needs of a particular church. This is another challenge to the Kenyan church leaders; they must train Christians for the works of service. The saints must be trained, because we fail them we appoint them to leadership positions or ask them to do works of service without training them. We see it as pathetic and disappointing when we hear church leaders complaining or accusing their junior staff in their organizations when we know that they have not taken the initiative to train them.

Message and Messenger

We have maintained in this book that, the life of a Christian leader cannot be separated from his or her leadership position. The Pauline model of leadership emphasizes the importance of spiritual, moral, mental, and family qualifications for Christian leaders. A leader is effective in leadership by influencing with his life those that he is leading. Our view is that the life of a Christian leader is what makes him/her effective. We find the church in Kenya inconsistent when she appoints leaders who do not qualify to be Christian leaders, because they do not have the necessary qualifications.

A Christian leader must be one who is beyond reproach, that is, one who cannot be laid upon or accused of anything which can cause reproach to his ministry of leadership (1 Tim. 3:2, Titus 1:6). Some ministries have grown when the leader meets this qualification, but others have not been effective when they choose leaders who do not have this qualification.

It is essential that a Christian leader be a husband of one wife. He must be one-wife sort of husband, and having no relationship beyond his marriage (1 Tim. 3:2, Titus 1:6). A Christian leader with relationships beyond her/his marriage should know he/she is biblically disqualified for Christian leadership.

A Christian leader must be sober, sound-minded, calm, temperate, opposed to any kind of excess, serious and sensible, dignified and orderly, and given to teaching and able to teach. All these qualifications emphasize that a leader's mental state and management ability are to be put into account in his/her leadership function (1 Tim. 3:2, Titus 1:7). We see a contradiction to this mental qualification when we see Christians whose integrity and sanity are questionable but are appointed to leadership positions. It is not a good testimony for Christian leaders who have been unable to control their tempers and thereby quarrel with other church leaders. This would contradict the biblical model presented in our thesis.

The leader's attitude and influence are to be considered in the appointment of Christian leaders (Tim. 3:3, Titus 1:7,8). A Christian leader must be a lover of guests and one who is fond of offering hospitality (1 Tim. 3:2, Titus 1:8). This qualification is not a difficult one in the Kenya setting because Kenyans love guests. Unfortunately, because of the Western influence to Africa socialism, by introducing individualism, monetary budgets, and time consciousness, this qualification must be still checked and seen in the Christian leader.

The Christian leader must be one who does not sit long hours at his wine cellar and become quarrelsome after drinking (1 Tim.

3:3, Titus 1:7,8). These portions of scripture cannot be used to mean 'total abstaining' from drinking of wine as many of our saints have done in Kenya. The issue here is that a Christian leader must not over-indulge in drinking of wine. A Christian leader must not be quick-tempered nor should he be contentious. He must be self-controlled, and thereby not hurt or injure saints by his contention or by his glorying in argument. A Christian leader must not be a lover of money. He must not be person whose aim in leading or in doing works of service is money. He must not be one who wishes to become rich 'soon.' This attitude increases corruption in the church.

Family Qualification

The family qualification expressed in 1 Tim. 3:4, 5, and Titus 1:6 must be met by every Christian leader. We are of the opinion that the leadership ministry depends on the life in the household. In most of the cases, success or failure in the home life of a Christian has a direct effect of the effectiveness of the Christian leadership ability. Therefore, a Christian leader must be one who manage's his household well. He must be able to bring his children to subjection and obedience. They must do this in relation to Christ as well as to their human father. When children are within the age bracket that allows them to be under the direct control of their father, then they must obey, respect, and be subject to his guidance. Some Christian leaders have been known to neglect their homes, including their marriage life and children. Other leaders have been known to have forgotten their spiritual responsibilities over their children. All Christian leaders must take caution on this.

Experience and growth in knowledge and love of Christ are important qualifications of a Christian leader (1 Tim. 3:6, Titus 1:9). A Christian leader must not be a new convert on whose intelligence (knowledge of the word) and solidarity (constancy) of Christian character has been approved. The sudden elevation of a new convert to leadership position can lead him to pride, conceit, and confusion. He must be known to be a firm holder of the Christian faith who leads his life in light of the revealed truth of the word of

God (9 1 Tim. 3:9, Titus 1:9). The high rate of church growth in Kenya has been given as a reason for elevation of new converts to leadership but the Pauline model leadership disapproves of this. Those who promote novices to leadership contradict this model.

A Leader in and Out of the World

A Christian leader lives in the world but does not belong to the world. He is not of this world but his leadership is ministry to the world. Therefore, he must be of good reputation or of good standing with those outside the church (1 Tim. 3:7). This will help one appointed to Christian leadership to be a blessing to the world. The church in Kenya is challenged to consider asking for recommendations from those outside the church before appointing men/women to leadership offices.

The issue of money scandals, misuse of church funds, or embezzling of church funds directly contradicts the Pauline model of church leadership. This model calls for church leaders who are beyond reproach, and who are not lovers of money. They should be honest and not lovers of base gain. This model calls for a decision to change from these evil practices or such a leader automatically disqualifies from church leadership.

The comparison of the Pauline Model of church leadership with the current scene of the church in Kenya shows that the church in Kenya has some weak points which need to be addressed as we try to meet the biblical model. We cannot overlook the fact that church leaders in Kenya have led many people to Christ. There are many strong points such as dedication and commitment of church leaders which has led to the growth of the church we see.

Modeling for Servant Leadership

Part Four: Epilogue

CHAPTER SIXTEEN

Summary and Conclusion

Brief Overview Model of Leadership in the New Testament

Leadership in the New Testament is service. It is servant-hood towards God and the recipients of the service. This calls for humble attitude to the person who is offering the service. Christian leadership is servant-hood and service (see Matt. 20:25-28, 23:11, 12, Luke 1:2, 2 Cor. 3:6, 1 Tim. 4:6, Eph. 4:12). Leadership in the New Testament is not the office but the person who is doing the leading. This means that the life of a Christian leader comes before the office he is holding, thus the servant-hood.

New Testament leadership is a ministry of nurturing, tending, shepherding, giving an example, guiding, teaching, and disciplining the church committed to the charge of the Christian leader. New Testament leadership is not without cost. It means sacrificing, self-denial, and not looking at the rights of the leader. The leader in most of the cases gives way because he leads the way. The church leader is a minister and not a master.

Brief Overview of Pauline Model of Leadership

The examination of 1 Tim. 3:1-16 and Titus 1:1-16 shows us clearly that leadership is the person leading. Paul therefore gave strict qualifications which are required of the church leader. The qualifying qualities are not just to be seen in a leader at the point of joining the leadership ministry but they are to continue in his daily life to leading. We also concluded that these qualifications are high standards which must be adhered to in all cases of appointing Christian leaders without exceptions or exemptions. Christian leadership involves the whole person, and all apartments and departments of his life-his inner (private) life and his outer (public) life-must be congruent and in agreement.

The examination of Ephesians 4:1-16 shows us that the church is one, despite the differences of minor details that have come through traditions. Church leaders must take pains to preserve that Christian Unity. The church is a Unity with diversity, and this calls for all Christians to use their diverse gifts for the glory of God and for the perfecting of the saints.

Recommendations and Critique

It is my sincere hope that any church leader who reads this book will do so carefully and thereby be able to measure himself or herself against the God-given standards that are discussed in the entire text. Chapter three which discusses the current scene in Kenya is written with the hope that church leaders will look at it, see where we need to put things right, and begin to take the necessary steps.

The qualifications and all other discussions that concern Christian leaders must be taken seriously. They must be considered by the church at large and implemented. It is my conviction that the church in Kenya must go into the word of God to understand and undertake the heavy tasks of church leadership. These heavy tasks of leadership must be taken with all seriousness by those who accept it. They must be eager to maintain their 'effectiveness' by maintaining the significance of the message and messenger part of the Christian servant leadership. Above all, Christ must be allowed to remain in control of the heart of a Christian leader as he seeks to serve in the African church.

Last but not least, the images of leadership in the early church, Western, Eastern and African church is male-oriented and male-dominated. As church leadership shifts to include women in leadership, the structures and contents of servant leadership must include women.

Recommended Bibliography

Church Growth
Arnett, Ronald C. *Dwell in Peace*, Elgin, Illinois,1980.
Barna, George, *Turn-Around Churches* .Venture, California: Regal Books, 1993.
Becker, Penny Edgell, *Congregations in Conflict: Cultural Models of Local Religious Life,* Cambridge: University Press, 1999.
Benson, Jr., Charles E. and Others, *In Praise of Congregations*, Cambridge, Massachusetts: Cowley Publications, 1999.
Brennan, Patrick J., *Re-Imaging the Parish*, New York: The Crossroad Publishing Company,1990.
Callahan, Kennon L. , *A New Beginning for Pastors and Congregations*, San Francisco, CA: Jossey-Bass, 1999.
Carey, George, *The Church in the Market Place*, Harrisburg, PA: Morehouse Publishing, 1985,1989.
Crabtree, Davida Foy, *The Empowering Church*.New York: The Alban Institute, 1989.
Doely, Sarah Bentley, Ed., *Women's Liberation and The Church*, New York: Association Press, 1970.
Dudley, Carl S. and Sally A. Johnson, *Energizing the Congregation*. Louisville, Kentucky: Westminster/John Knox Press,1993.
Dulles, Avery, *Models of the Church,* Expanded Edition, New York: Doubleday Image Books, 1974, 1987.
Harris, John C., Stress, *Power and Ministry: An Approach to the Current Dilemmas of Pastors and Congregations*, New York: The Alban Institute, 1977.

Hawkins, Thomas R., *The Learning Congregation: A New Vision of Leadership*, Louisville, Kentucky, 1977.

Jenson, Ron and Jim Stevens, *Dynamics of Church Growth*, Grand Rapids, Michigan: Baker Book House, 1981.

Kemper, Robert G., *Beginning A New Pastorate*, Nashville: Abingdon Press, 1978.

Kim, Young-IL, Ed., *Knowledge, Attitude and Experience: Ministry in the Cross-Cultural Context,* Nashville: Abingdon Press, 1992.

Levin, Pamela, Cycles of Power: *A User's Guide to The Seven Seasons of Life*, Deerfield Beach, Florida: Healthy Communications, Inc.,1988.

Ludwig, Glenn E., *In It For the Long Hall: Building Effective Long-Term Pastorates,* New York: The Alban Institute, 2002.

Lutz, Robert R. and Bruce T. Taylor, Eds., *Surviving in Ministry: Navigating the Pitfall, Experiencing the Renewal,* New York: Paulist Press, 1990.

McGavran, Donald A. and Winfield C. Arn, *Ten Steps for Church Growth* San Francisco: Harper & Row Publishers, 1977.

Pattison, E. Mansell, *Pastor and Parish*, Philadelphia: Fortress Press, 1977.

Randall, Robert L., *The Eternal Triangle: Pastor, Spouse and Congregation*, Minneapolis: Fortress Press, 1999.

Schaller, Lyle E. , *Activating the Passive Church: Diagnosis and Treatment*, Nashville, TN.: Abingdon Press,1981.

Sedgwick, Timothy F., *The Making of Ministry,* Boston, Massachusetts: Cowley Publications, 1993.

Steinke, Peter L. , *How Your Church Family Works: Understanding Congregations as Emotional Systems*, New York: The Alban Institute, 1993.

_____ , *Healthy Congregations: A Systems Approach*, New York: The Alban Institute, 1996.

Sellon, Mary K. and Others, *Redeveloping the Congregation: A How To for Lasting Change*, New York: The Alban Institute, 2002.

Stott, John R.W., Edited by C. B. Peter, Jane Gitau and Esther Mombo, *The Church in the New Millennium*, Eldoret, Kenya: Zapf Chancery, 2002.

Westerhoff III, John H., Living *The Faith Community: The Church that Makes a Difference,* san Francisco, Harper & Row Publishers, 1985.

Villa-Vicencio, Charles and John De Gruchy, Eds., *Resistance and Hope*, Grand Rapids, Michigan, Wm. B. Eerdmans, 1985.

Biblical Leadership

Abbot, T. K. *International Critical Commentary: Epistles to the Ephesians and to the Colossians.* Edinburgh: T. and T. Clark, 1979.

Adams, Arthur Merrihew. *Effective Leadership for Today's Church.* Philadephia: The Westminister Press, 1978.

Anderson, James D. and Jones, Ezra E. *The Management of Ministry.* San Francisco: Harper & Row Publishers, 1978.

Anderson, Robert C. *The Effective Pastor.* Chicago: Moody press, 1985.

Armerding, Hudson T. *Leadership.* Wheaton, Illinois: Tyndale House Publishers, 1978.

Barbers, Cyril J., and Strauss, Garry H. *Leadership: The Dynamics of Success.* Greenwood, S. C.: The Attic press, 1982.

Barth, Markus. *Ephesians.* Garden City, New York: Doubleday and Company, 1960.

Barkhof, L. *Systematic Theology.* Grand Rapids, Michigan: The Banner of Truth Trust, 1941.

Blaiklock, E. M. *The pastoral Epistles.* Grand Rapids, Michigan: Zondervan Publishing House, 1972.

Buswell, J. Oliver. *A Systematic Theology of the Christian Religion*. Grand Rapids, Michigan: Zondervan publishing House, 1962.

Bridges, Charles. *The Christian Ministry*. London: The Banner of Truth, 1961.

Brown, Colin, ed. *The New International Dictionary of New Testament Theology*. 3 vols. Devon: The Paternoster Press Ltd., 1975.

Bruce, Alexander Balmain. *The Expositor's Greek Testament*. 5 vols. Grand Rapids, Michigan: William B. Eerdmans Publishing Company, 1980.

Chafer, Lewis Sperry. *Major Bible Themes*. Grand Rapids, Michigan: Zondervan publishing House, 1974.

Charley, Julian. *50 key words of the Bible*. London: Lutterworth Press, 1971.

Dayton, Edward R., and Engstrom, Ted. W. *Strategy for Leadership*. New Jersey: Fleming H. Revell Company, 1979.

Dibelius, Martin and Conzelmann, Hans. *Pastoral Epistles*. Translated by Philip Buttolph and Adela Yarbro. Philadelphia: Fortress, 1972.

Dictionary of New Testament Theology Vol.3, s. v. "Serve, Deacon, Worship," by K. Hess

Douglass, Stephen B. *Managing Yourself*. San Bernarda California: Here's Life Publishers, 1978.

Dougla, J. D. *The New Bible Dictionary*. London: Inter-Varsity Press, 1962.

_____. *The New International Dictionary of the Christian Church*. Devon: The Paternoster Press, 1978.

Eadie, John. *Commetary on the Epistle to the Ephesians*. Grand Rapids, Michigan: Zondervan publishing House, 1955.

Eastern, Burton Scott. *The pastoral Epistles – Introduction Translation, Commentary and Word Studies*. London: SCM Press, 1948.

Eims, Leroy, *Be the Leader You Were Meant To Be*. Wheaton: SP Publications, 1975.

Engstrom, Ted W. and Dayton, Edward R. *The Art of Management for Christian Leaders*. Waco Texas: Word Books Publisher, 1976.

Engstrom, Ted W. *The Making of a Christian Leader*. Grand Rapids, Michigan: Zondervan Publishing House, 1976.

Evans, William. *The Great Doctrines of the Bible*. Chicago: Moody Press, 1974.

Foulkes, Francis, Ephesians. Leicester, England: Inter-Varsity Press, 1963

_____. *Fight the Good Fight-study Guide to 1 Timothy*. London: Cox and Wyman Limited, 1971.

Gangel, Kenneth O. *So You Want to be a Leader*. Harrisburg: Christian Publications, 1975.

_____. *Competent to Lead*. Chicago: Moody Press, 1974.

Grassi, Joseph A. *The Secret of Paul the Apostle*. Maryknoll, New Orbis Books, 1970.

Green, Michael. *Called to serve*. London: Hodder and Stoughton Limited, 1964.

Green, Oliver B. *The Epistle of Paul the Apostle to the Ephesians*. Greenville, South Carolina: The Gospel Hour, Inc., 1963.

Guthrie, Donald. *The Letter to the Hebrews: An Introduction and Commentary*. Grand Rapids, Michigan: William B. Eerdmans Publishing Company, 1983.

_____. *The Pastoral Epistles*. Leicester, England: Inter-Varsity Press, 1957.

Hanson, Anthony Tyrrell. *Studies in the Pastoral Epistles* London: S.P.C.K., 1968.

Hendriksen, William. *New Testament Commentary – Exposition of the Pastoral Epistles*. Grand Rapids, Michigan Baker Book House, 1957.

_____. New *Testament Commentary-Exposition of Ephesians.* Grand Rapids, Michigan: Baker Book House, 1967.

Hendrix, Olan. *Management for the Christian Leader.* Milford, Michigan: Mott Media Press, 1976.

Hodges, Melvin L. *The Indigenous Church.* Sprigfield, Missouri: Gospel Publishing House, 1976.

Hyde, Douglas. *Dedication and Leadership.* Notre Dame, Indians: University of Notre Dame Press, 1966.

International Standard Bible Encylopedia, s. v. "Pastor," by W. R. Harris.

Jenson, Ron, and Stevens, Jim. *Dynamics of Church Growth.* Grand Rapids, Michigan: Baker Book Housing Company, 1981.

Johnson, George, ed. *Ephesian, Philippinas, Colossians and Philemon.* London: Thomas Nelson and Sons Ltd, 1967.

Kent, Homer A. *The Pastoral Epistles – Studies in 1 and 2 Timothy and Titus.* Chicago: Moody Press, 1958.

Kilinski, Kenneth K, and Wofford, Jerry C. *Organsation and Leadership in the Local Church.* Grand Rapids, Michigan: Zondervan Publishing House, 1973.

Ladd, George Eldon. *A Theology of the New Testament.* Grand Rapids, Michigan: William B. Eerdmans Publishing Company. 1974.

Leas, Sped and Kittlaus, Paul. *Church Fights.* Philadelphia: The Westminister Press, 1973.

Lloyd-Jones, D. M. *Christian Unity: An Exposition of Ephesians 4:1-16.* Carlisle, Pennsylvania: The Banner of Truth Trust, 1980.

Macquarrie, John. *Principles of Christian Theology.* London: SCM Press Ltd., 1966.

Marshall, 1. Howard. *The Acts of the Apostles: An Introduction and commentary.* Grand Rapids, Michigan: William B. Eerdmans Publishing Company, 1980

McGavran, Donald A., and Arn, Winfield C. *The Steps for Church Growth*. New York: Harper and Row Publishers, 1977.

Nicoll, W. Robert., ed. *The Expositor's Greek Testament*. Grand Rapids, Michigan: William B. Eerdmans Publishing Company, 1980.

Oates, Wayne E. *The Christian Pastor*. Philadelphia: The Westminster Press, 1951.

Russell, Antony. *The Clerical Profession*. London: S.P.C.K., 1980.

Richards, Larry, and Getz, Gene. "A Biblical Style of Leadership." *Leadership 2* (spring 1981): 68-78.

Richards, Lawrence O., and Hoeldtke, Clyde. *A Theology of Church Leadership*. Grand Rapids, Michigan: Zondervan Publishing House, 1980.

Ryrie, Charles Caldwell. *Balancing the Christian Life*. Chicago: Moody Press, 1969.

Sanders, J. Oswald. *Spiritual Leadership*. Chicago: Moody Press, 1967.

Saucy, Robert L. *The Church in God's program*. Chicago: Moody Press, 1972.

Stibbs, Alan M. and Walls, Andrew F. *The First Epistle General of Peter – an Introduction and Commentary*. Grand Rapids Michigan: William B. Eerdmans Publishing Company, 1983.

Stott, John R. W. Gurd the Gospel: *Message of 2 Timothy*. London: Inter-Varsity Press, 1973.

_____. *God's New Society-The Message of Ephesians*. Leicester, England: Inter-Varsity Press, 1979.

Tasker, R. V. G. *The General Epistle of James: An Introduction and Commentary*. Grand Rapids, Michigan: William B. Eerdmans Publishing Company, 1983.

Thiessen, Henry C. *Lectures in Systematic Theology*. Grand Rapids, Michigan: William B. Eerdmans Publishing Company, 1949.

Turnbull, Ralph G., ed. *Baker's Dictionary of Practical Theology*. Grand Rapids, Michigan: Baker Book House Company, 1961.
Vine, W. E. *Vine's Expository Dictionary of New Testament Words*. Mclean, Virginia: Macdonald Publishing Company, 1940.
Wuest, Kenneth S. Wuest's *Word Studies. 3 vols*. Grand Rapids, Michigan: William B. Eerdmans Publishing Company, 1950.
Zondervan Topical Bible, s.v. " Minister, "By Edward Viening *Zondervan Pictorial Encyclopedia of the Bible*, s.v. "Servant," by J. R. Michaels.
Zondervan Pictorial Encyclopedia of the Bible, s. v. "Service," By G. B. Fundeburk. *Zondervan Pictorial Encyclopedia of the Bible*, s. v. "Ministry," By R. A. Bodey.

Africa in General

Berman, EdwardH. *African Reactions to Missionary Education*. New York: Teachers College Press, 1975.
Bond, George; Johnson, Walton; and Walkers, Sheila s., eds. *African Christianity*. New York: Academic Press, 1979.
Falk, Peter. *The Growth of the Church in Africa*. Grand Rapids, Michigan: Zondervan Publishing House, 1979.
Hildebrandt, Jonathan. *History of the Church in Africa*. Achimota, Ghana: Africa Christian Press, 1981.
Jules-Rossette, Bernnetta., ed. *The New Religions of Africa*. New Jersey: Ablex Publishing Corporation. 1979.
Kato, Byang H. *Theological Pitfalls in Africa*. Kisumu: Evangel Publishing House, 1975.
Kendall, Elliott. *The End of an Era – Africa and the Missionary*. London: SPCK, 1978.
Mbiti, John S. *The Crisis of Mission in Africa*. Mukono, Uganda: Uganda Church Press, 1971.
Parrinder, Geoffrey. *Religion in an African City*. London: Oxford University Press, 1953.

Shoter, Aylward. *African Christian Spirituality*. Maryknoll, New York: Orbis Books, 1978.
Taber, Charles R., ed. *The Church in Africa 1977*. California: William Carey Library, 1978.
_____. *African Culture and the Christian Church*. London: Cassel Ltd, 1973.
Wakatama, Pius. *Independence for the Third World Church* Illinois: Inter-Varsity Press, 1976.

East Africa and Kenya

A.I.C., *1st Anniversary of the Africa Inland Church*. Kijabe: Africa Inland Church Press, 1972.
Anderson, William B. Man *Facing Out*. Nairobi, Kenya: Uzima Press Ltd., 1977.
Anderson, William B. *The Church in East Africa 1840 – 1974*. Dodoma: Central Tanganyika Press, 1977.
Barrett, David B., Mambo, George K; Mclaughlin, Janice; and McVeigh, Malcolm J. *Kenya Church Handbook*. Kisumu: Evangel Publishing House, 1973.
Barrett, David B. *World Christian Encyclopedia: A Comparative Survey of Churches and Religions in the Modern World* A.D. 1900 – 2000. Nairobi: Oxford University Press, 1982.
Cassidy, Michael and Osei-Mensah. *Together in one place*. Nairobi, Kenya: Evangel Publishing House, 1978.
Cassidy, Michael and Verlinden, Luc. *Facing the New Challenges*. Kisumu, Kenya: Evangel Publishing House, 1978.
Cavicchi, Edmondo. *Problems of Change in Kikuyu Tribal Society* Bologna, Italy: E. M. I., 1977.
Kariuki, Obadia. *A Bishop Facing Mount Kenya*. Nairobi, Kenya: Uzima Press Ltd., 1985. *Kenya, Constitution of* (1969).
Kenyatta, Jomo. *Harambee: Prime Ministers Speeches*. Nairobi, Kenya: Oxford University Press, 1964.

Langrey, Myrtle and Kiggins, Tom. *A Serving People.* Nairobi: Oxford University Press, 1974.

Leo, Christopher. *Land and Class in Kenya.* Toronto: University of Toronto Press, 1984.

Macpherson, R. *The Presbyterian Church in Kenya.* Nairobi: Kenya Litho Ltd., 1970.

Miller, Paul M. *Equipping for Ministry.* Tanzania: Central Tanganyika Press, 1969.

Miano, J. M. *Hyenas in the Church.* Nairobi: Uzima Press Ltd.,

Murray-Brown, Jeremy. *Kenyatta.* London: Fontana and Colons, 1972.

National Christian Council of Kenya. *A Christian View of Politics in Kenya.* Nairobi, Kenya: Uzima Press Ltd., 1983.

Nthamburi, Zablon John. *A History of the Methodist Church in Kenya.* Nairobi: Uzima Press Ltd, 1982.

Ogot, Bethwell A. *Historical Dictionary of Kenya.* London: The Scarecrow Press, 1981.

_____. *Politics and Nationalism in Colonial Kenya.* Nairobi, Kenya: East African Publishing House, 1972.

Ojuka, Aloo and Ochieng, William, ed. *Politics and Leadership in Kenya.* Nairobi, Kenya: East Africa Literature Bureau, 1975.

Okullu, Henry. *Church and State in National Building and Human Development.* Nairobi: Uzima Press Ltd., 1984.

_____. *Church and Politics in East Africa.* Nairobi: Uzima Press Ltd., 1974.

Republic of Kenya. Ministry of Finance and Planning. Central Bureau of Statistics. *Economic Survey 1984,* May 1984.

Republic of Kenya. Ministry of Economic Planning and National Development. Central Bureau of Statistics. *Economic Survey 1986,* May 1986.

Republic of Kenya. Ministry of Economic Planning and National Development. Central Bureau of Statistics. *Social*

Perspectives: Literacy in Rural Kenya, 1980/81, vol. 7 No. 1 December 1982.

Journals, Newspapers, and Papers

Anderson, Robert. "Christians and the State." The *Weekly Review*, 3 August 1984, p. 21.

Billinglysley, Lloyd. "I Preach Money." *Eternity* (February 1986): 27-31.

Bubna, Don. "Ten Reasons Not to Resign." *Leadership* 4 (Fall 1983): 4-80.

Burnham, Monty; Egmont, Westy; Hagstrom, Richard; Macdonald, Gerdon; and Torms, Paul. "Leadership Forum. Conflict: Facing it in Yourself and in your Church. *Leadership* (Spring 1980): 15-28.

Buzzard, Lynn. "War and Peace in the Local Church." *Leadership* (Summer 1983): 21-30.

Carson, D. A. "The Doctrinal Causes of Division in our Churches." *The Banner of Truth* 218 (November 1981): 7-19.

Carson, H. M. "Guidance for Ministers." Banner of Truth 217 (October 1981): 19-25.

Carson, Herbert. "Overseers of the Church." *The Banner of Truth 222* (March 1982): 8-16.

Djongwe, Rene Daidansoma. "The Role of the Local Pastor and Church in Development." *Evangelical Ministries 5* (January-April 1986): 8.

Gary, Gary. "Withering Away Leadership." *The Clergy Journal* (April 1986): 36-37.

Getz, Gene. "Sharpening the Pastor's Focus." *Leadership 6* (Summer 1985): 12-19.

Gonzales, Gary; Rouner, Arthur A.; Lemon, Cal; Knudsen, Chilton; Atha, Grayson and Larson, L. Jonathan. "Anatomy of a Church Fight." *Leadership* 4 (Summer 1983): 96-103.

Henderson, Authur. "Leadership in the Churches." *The Journal of the Christian Brethren Research Fellowship* 30 (1980): 70-72.

Kachur, Robert M. and Neff, David. "Surviving Leadership in Fast Forward." *Christianity Today* (April 1986): 22-26.

Litfin, A. Duane. "The Nature of the Pastoral Role: The Leader as Completer." *Bibliotheca Sacra* 139 (January-March 1982): 57-66.

_____. "An Under Shepherd." *The Banner of Truth* 220 (January 1982): 11-18.

Ngw'eno, Hilary. "Grace Alum: The Confidence Woman." *The Weekly Review*, 21 January 1983, pp. 13-26.

_____. "Election Controversy." *The Weekly Review*, 22 June, 1984, 11-12.

_____. "A Sensitive Issue." *The Weekly Review*, 22 June, 1984, 13.

_____. "Scathing Attack." *The Weekly Review*, 22 June, 1984, 13-14.

_____. "Exposing the Rift." *The Weekly Review*, 29 June, 1984, 10-11.

_____. "A Question of Who should Be Prayed For." *The weekly Review*, 27 July, 1984, 3-11.

_____. "More Wrangles." *The Weekly Review*, 17 August 1984, 10.

_____. "No Let Up." *The Weekly Review*, 21 September 1984, 11.

_____. "Mending Fences: PCEA Leaders Pay Visit to State House." *The Weekly Review*, 19 October 1984, 14.

_____. "Minor Storm: PCEA Suspends Rungiri Pastor." *The Weekly Review*, 5 October 1984, 13-16.

_____. "Enter the AG: Muli Lays Down the Rule Regarding Churches." *The Weekly Review*, 5 October 1984, 13.

_____. "Catholics Criticize Sterilization Clinics." *The Weekly Review*, 16 November 1984, 4-9.

_____. "No More New Churches." *The Weekly Review,* 9 November 1984, 13-15.

_____. "Fun to Come: PCEA Elections in April Promise Plenty of Interest." *The Weekly Review*, 4 January 1985, 9-10.

_____. "Revived Wrangles: Attempts to Prevent Metto Taking Part in Church Function." *The Weekly Review*, 22 February 1985, 12.

_____. "Church and Politics Wrangle in Eldoret." *The Weekly Review,* 29 March 1985, 4-5.

_____. "Long Standing Differences." *The Weekly Review*, 29 March 1985, 6-7.

Zapf Chancery Tertiary Level Publications (Continued)

Auditing Priniples: A Stuents' Handbook by Musa O. Nyakora (2007)*The Concept of* Botho *and HIV/AIDS in Botswana* edited by Joseph B. R. Gaie and Sana K. MMolai (2007)
Captive of Fate: A Novel by Ketty Arucy (2007)
A Guide to Ethics by Joseph Njino (2008)
Pastoral Theology: Rediscovering African Models and Methods by Ndung'u John Brown Ikenye (2009)
The Royal Son: Balancing Barthian and African Christologies by Zablon Bundi Mutongu (2009)
AIDS, Sexuality, and Gender: Experiencing of Women in Kenyan Universities by Nyokabi Kamau (2009)
Modern Facilitation and Training Methodology: A Guide to Best Practice in Africa by Frederick Chelule (2009)
How to Write a Winning Thesis by Simon Kang'ethe et al (2009)
Absolute Power and Other Stories by Ambrose Rotich Keitany (2009)
Y'sdom in Africa: A Personal Journey by Stanley Kinyeki (2010)
Abortion and Morality Debate in Africa: A Philosophical Enquiry by George Kegode (2010)
The Holy Spirit as Liberator: A Study of Luke 4: 14-30 by Joseph Koech (2010)
Biblical Studies, Theology, Religion and Philosophy: An Introduction for African Universities, Gen. Ed. James N. Amanze (2010)
Modeling for Servant-Leaders in Africa: Lessons from St. Paul by Ndung'u John Brown Ikenye (2010)